GROWING PAINS AND GAINS

The Way it Was

Growing Up

In

Small Town Jefferson, Georgia

by

Harry Woodward Bryan

Order this book online at www.trafford.com
or email orders@trafford.com

Most Trafford titles are also available at major online book retailers.

Note for Librarians: A cataloguing record for this book is available from Library
and Archives Canada at www.collectionscanada.ca/amicus/index-e.html

Printed in Victoria, BC, Canada.

ISBN: 978-1-4269-0493-6

Trafford rev. 10/13/2009

www.trafford.com

North America & international
toll-free: 1 888 232 4444 (USA & Canada)
phone: 250 383 6864 ♦ fax: 812 355 4082

Contents

THIS BOOK IS DEDICATED to the memory of my parents William 'Bill' Thomas Bryan, Jr. and Frances Lelia (Woodward) Bryan and to the memory of my brother William 'Billy' Thomas Bryan, 111. And to the honor of my sister Frances Woodward (Bryan) Kelly and my brother John Proctor Bryan and to my good friends C. B. Lord and the late Henry Allen, who were like brothers to me.

A very special honor goes to my wife of fifty four years, Jayne (Staton) Bryan for her patience, understanding and guidance. Without her this book would not have been possible.

To the many who were there for us when growing up, especially our older neighbors and friends. A special thanks to John Anderson, Wylie McEver and the late Willie Craig whose escapades with me left many happy memories.

******

Looking Back

Looking back to the days gone by
Is a nostalgic and fun thing to do.
Pausing to remember families and friends
And sometimes the mischief, too.
Lessons were learned and values taught
That made us strong,
Eager and ready to live our lives,
seeking right from wrong.

Acknowledgements

9/ Remembrances: The Depression years by Marie Staton Massey

10/ Jefferson High School and Football - Their beginning by Harry W. Bryan-March 2001.

11/ Encyclopedia of Georgia Biography – Volume 1, 1931: by Lucian Lamar Knight -State Historian of Georgia, Emeritus and The Story of Georgia – Biographical Volume - 1938

12/ Athens, Ga. Banner Herald 1916

13/ Apple Valley information furnished by Douglas "Ponchie" Beck: Georgia Place-Names by Kenneth Krabow, 1975 and J. T. and Jacque Wilkes

14/ Tennessee Valley Authority Quad –Dillard Quadrangle: 168 N. W. - Georgia. & North Carolina.

15/ Remembrances: Coach Hardin 1943/44 to 1945/46 school years by J. T. Wilkes

16/ 1950 U. S. census as reported by Wikipedia, the free Encyclopedia – 17th United States census.

17/ Account of the discovery of the Martin Institute fire by Bob Freeman.

18/ A partial history of the Jackson County Academy and Martin Institute; The Jackson Herald January 15, 1942 - Vol. 67 No. 30

19/ An expanded history of the first site of the Jackson County Academy and Martin Institute by Jayne Staton Bryan

20/ "The Jeffersonian" – 1950 Jefferson High School yearbook.

21/ Beth Laughinghouse – Better Hometown Manager.

22/ The Banner Herald-February 3, 1985; written by Masie

Underwood; Classic Scene Editor

23/ Family history notes; Harry W. Bryan

24/ Georgia Alumni Record by T. W. Reed: A tribute to the
memory of Dr. J. P. Proctor

Note: A special thank you to Bob Freeman for his permission
to use his historical photographs of downtown Jefferson and
to Beth Laughinghouse for the use of the Crawford W. Long
Collection of photographs of historical places.

Introduction

GROWING PAINS --- AND GAINS

Jefferson, Georgia – a sleepy little town and as the
saying goes, "was put to sleep in 1842 by Doctor
Crawford W. Long upon his discovery of ether as an
anesthetic, and it never woke up."

IN THE 1930S AND 1940s the population of our fair city was said
to be about 1,500 people, all within three fourths of a mile radius
from the middle of the square. As we begin the 21st century the
town limits have been stretched to take in this and that and the
folks from the Atlanta area and other places are rapidly moving
in. Our sleepy little town is beginning to yawn and show some
serious signs of awakening, much to the chagrin of some and
much to the favor of others, I being one of the some. Change and
I just somehow do not get along. We never have and most likely
never will but as it has been said many times, change is inevitable
and we either accept it or wither in its wake.

With these forthcoming words I have attempted to reminisce
the olden days, my days and those of Brother Billy 'Bill,' C. B.
'Buck' Lord, Thomas McMullen and a few others. Some have

moved away, some have passed away and some never left. Those were the days when neighbor knew neighbor and we just seemed to all grow up together. We had what we had and there was not much more to want. They were the days before air conditioning when fresh air poured through the screened windows and doors and the steady hum of the electric fan could be heard in most homes. It was the days before we were captivated by television. The radio and record player were the king of entertainment and the family would gather around to hear the big band music and listen to their all time favorite programs. I recall programs like: Edgar Burgen and Charlie McCarthy, Amos and Andy, Jack Benny and Rochester, Mister District Attorney, The Lone Ranger, the Shadow, the Hit Parade and many others. It was a time when neighbors would just drop in to visit or maybe to borrow a cup of sugar or a stick of butter and an egg or two.

I remember sitting and swinging on our porch on a summer's night and neighbors taking casual walks would stop for a cordial visit. Things were so simple and we knew and trusted everyone. Billy, C. B. and I would camp out in our side yard with no thought of harm coming to us. On one occasion as we camped out, C. B. did a little sleep walking and ended up sleeping in the middle of the street. Luckily Doctor Lord had a night call and found him, curled up and peaceably sleeping. He stopped and gently put him on the back seat of his car and went about his mission. C. B. did not remember a thing but Billy and I were puzzled as to what happened to him. Most folk left their houses unlocked at night and even when they went away for short visits and no one hardly ever took the keys out of their cars.

I shall never forget the sounds of the night while lying in bed on a sultry, summer night. I remember the hum of a hungry mosquito that had managed somehow to get through the screened window causing Billy and me to hastily pull the sheet over our heads. I remember hearing the courthouse clock strike the early morning hours of the peaceful night and the barn owls clicking and screeching as they flew from the courthouse clock tower on their night's hunt. To hear the coal fired locomotive steam engine puffing along on the Gainesville Midland Railroad, blowing its steam whistle at each distant and nearby crossing was a beautiful sound. I could hear the clanging of its cars as it switched off of the main line to chug over the short trestle passing Fite's cotton gin and on to the old depot. The train can still be heard but now is powered by a diesel engine and the chugging and puffing of the old engine is replaced with a continuous, monotonous, groaning roar. Young and old could never forget the sound of the shrill mill whistle blowing in the early morning hours alerting the workers of the shift change. Now the old mill is quiet but still stands as a reminder of the bygone years. Another nighttime memory was the quick flash of the Arcade Airport beacon light as it rotated 360 degrees during its night's vigil, giving notice of its location.

All are gone now except the striking of the courthouse clock and the screech of an occasional barn owl, should one happen to be outside after dark to hear, reminding one of the once peaceful and simple times. But now, the impurity of the air and noise of the endless traffic almost mandates us to close the doors and windows of our homes and turn on the air conditioners and television that completely separate us from the once stillness of the peaceful night.

We all have our thoughts and experiences of how it was back then – these are my thoughts and remembrances of how it was for four boys growing up in the 1930s, 1940s and 1950s. Our experiences, some industrious and ambitious, some leaning on the edge of danger, some mischievous and yes, some are even regrettable. But all helped us to build a life of character and integrity. Guided by the many wonderful people in our lives, especially our parents who through loving care and in some cases hard love built the framework for our years of adulthood.

Some names have been deleted or changed to protect the innocent and to eliminate any undue embarrassment that might be caused by a particular incident. All stories are based on true happenings as remembered.

Chapter One

Our Town-The Way it Was

Chapter one

JEFFERSON, GEORGIA - THE county seat of Jackson County was just a simple small town, not unlike many small southern towns. The first courthouse was located south of the town square and later around 1817 was relocated to the center of the square. Because of the muddy mire of the unpaved streets the courthouse was torn down and rebuilt in 1879 on its present location.1/ The square was much larger then but in recent years has been reduced to a median. The streets were dotted with beautiful elm trees and oak trees and shrubbery was on the square. The city was built to meet the needs of the people and all the basic needs were there. Smith's Hardware furnished tools, cut glass, sold hunting ammunition, knives and all sort of things. Moore and Ellington's Drug Store furnished medicines for curing the sick, castor oil included, and a soda fountain for refreshing the citizens. Doctor Lord said, "castor oil was only good for greasing wagon wheels" and I think we can all agree with that. I shall never forget the cherry smashes and the sodas of all flavors. Mr. Moore, or Dud as he was called, would tire of people wanting water, especially the kids and occasionally would fill their glasses with carbonated water. He would get a good, knee-slapping laugh out of that.

The Roosevelt Theater and later the Joy Theater entertained the citizens before the days of television. It was quite an event when "Gone With the Wind" was shown at the theater. It drew crowds like we had never seen before. The Joy Theater and Soda Shop opened in the late 1940s but the theaters were soon stripped of their popularity by television's stronghold on society and closed in the mid to late 1950s.

Many needs were met at Kesler's Five and Dime Store. They sold sewing needs to the ladies, school supplies for the children, bb shots for the hunters of the time and small glass pipes that we used for smoking corn silk and rabbit tobacco. Those things really got hot, too hot to handle most times.

The favorite eatery at the time was Pinson's Café. The café and telephone office were in the same building located on the site that is now the Pocket Park recently established by the Better Hometown Committee. Later in the 1940s Buck Marlowe purchased the Café and it became Marlow's Cafe. The newspaper of the day was the Jackson Herald and as the town character T. C. Morrison once said, "You can read the Jackson Herald, eat at Marlow's Café and go to bed with nothing on your mind and nothing in your stomach."

3

The Harrison Hotel was the focal point of Jefferson for many years. It was built in the 1800s to accommodate weary travelers traveling by stagecoach or horseback. The stagecoach driver would signal the number of passengers on board by the number of blasts from its horn. The hotel was said to be in such poor condition, that to repair it would cost a fortune. It was demolished in 1956 and replaced with a modern motel to upgrade the appearance of the town. It did not turn out as planned and is definitely an eye sore now.

One bank served the community and kept the wheels of commerce turning. Two cotton firms served the farmers by buying and/or storing their cotton and selling them fertilizer for next year's crop. Snuggled between the Moore and Ellington Drug Store and the Jackson Herald was the Jefferson Motor Company and on the other side of the Jackson Herald was Mr. Ed Kelly's Garage and in the late forties Mr. David Hardy's frozen food vault. Next was the City Hall and Fire department. On the corner at the juncture of the Athens highway was Mr. Tom Turner's Gas Station and later Godfrey's Standard Service Station was located there.

Mr. Ed Kelly worked on everything and most anything, from bicycles, tricycles to roller skates, to guns and cars. If it broke he could fix it. His customers ranged in age from four to a hundred and ten and you could ask him, "can you fix it Mr. Ed?" and his reply was always, "Eh! don't know, got to look at it first." Then he fixed it. He always had or made time to fix whatever we needed. I always enjoyed brief visits with Mr. Ed when Jayne and I returned home on weekend visits and vacations. He seemed to always be interested in the pine beetle infestations throughout the south, being afraid that they would be the demise of the southern pines. Mr. Ed was a special family friend and role model.

There were very few automobiles in the early days and many of the ladies did not bother to learn to drive. They did not see the need and got along pretty well without that convenience. Everything was in easy walking distance but for those ladies who were unable to get about or just wanted home delivery simply called Carl Legg's or Luke Lyle's Grocery Stores and their needs were promptly met. Most purchased their groceries on credit and Mr. Carl had his way of constantly reminding the customer of money due with this apparently effective short notation printed on the back of each delivery ticket:

"You need your money and I need mine.
If we could both have ours it would sure be fine.
But if you get yours and keep mine too.
What in the world am I going to do?" 2/

Just behind the First National Bank and facing Gordon Street was J. W. Massey's grocery store.3/Across the street on the corner was the Five and Dime Store. I shall never forget entering the grocery store through a flimsy screen door that hardly covered the opening when it was closed. Houseflies were abundant in those days and seemed to be more of a pest rather than a health hazard. That is the way it seemed to little boys anyway. Mr. Massey had a pickle barrel just to the right as you entered and it always had a weird appeal to me. I would stick my hand in the barrel and usually got a firm smack on the back of my hand from Dad.

Dad would buy salted mackerel. The mackerel was packed in salt brine in wooden buckets and was so salty it would almost blister your tongue. One time Dad bought a bucket and carried it to Rabun Gap on our summer vacation. The mackerel was tainted and made Dad sick. I always figured that was his just due for smacking my hand when I reached in the pickle barrel. Just kidding, but who knows?

The telephone system was pretty simple. Before the dial phone, one just lifted the receiver, gave a short ring and the pleasant voice of the operator said, "number please?" A number had two to four digits. Our home number was 158 and Dad's office was 43. It was a one on one situation so you had to be careful what you said because the operator could be listening. I remember answering the phone and the operator saying, "long distance call for Mr. Bryan" and if he was not home the operator would respond, "please have him call operator five," or whatever number she was, "thank you." I also remember when Jayne and I were dating, if we did not see each other we talked on the phone. Dad would call and tell the operator, "Pearl, tell Harry I need to talk to his Mother." Pearl would interrupt us and I would call Mother to the phone. Pretty simple but it got the job done.

Doctor Lord and Doctor Stovall made house calls and traveled throughout the county checking on their patients, foregoing the patient coming to see them. We did not bother making appointments as we just dropped in and our needs were met.

Doctor Lord's office was in the small building located between the Miss Ossie Smith's Boarding House and the Old Roosevelt Theater. Doctor Stovall's office was in Doctor Crawford Long's old office, now a part of the Crawford Long Museum.

Doctor Lord's Office: first floor

Jayne tells the story of the day when she and Shirley came home from school and her throat felt scratchy. She looked into the mirror and seeing bumps at the back of her tongue said frantically, "Shirley! I have to go see Doctor Lord, there are bumps on my tongue!" Her parents were not at home at the time so off they went. No patients were in the office and after explaining to Nancy Daniel, Doctor Lord's receptionist and nurse, she took her straight back to the good Doctor. Doctor Lord with his usual gentle manner looked into her mouth and said, "uh huh young lady you certainly do have bumps on your tongue and I can take them off if you want but you will not be able to taste anything, ever again." Simple times, simple ways, that's the way it was.

A popular place was Joe Baxter's General Store. We called it "general" because Mr. Joe would sell "bout anything that was not nailed to the floor." Mr. Baxter's Store was south of the square facing Lee Street and lay between the Old Post Office and Robinson's Shoe Store and Repair Shop. The Post Office was on the corner across from the present Subway. Next to Robinson's and on the corner was Kesler's Five and Dime Store.

Cigarettes were about twelve cents a pack and Mr. Baxter would break a pack and sell them for a penny each. Eight cents more per pack was quite a profit. A penny was pretty important in those days and would buy a lot of items. Mr. Baxter died a wealthy man and his legacy lives on through endowments and grants to various institutions and organizations.

Mr. Claude Robinson's Shoe Shop was a special place also. The smell of raw leather was always there as one walked in and the whirrrrrring of the stitching machine or the tapping of the Cobbler's tack hammer could be heard even before one entered the shop. It was a full service shoe store where half soles were common, heels were repaired and re-dying old shoes to refurbish them was commonplace. It is an amazing thing that conservation was a way of life during our growing up days but now waste has become common and seems to drive our economy. There seems to be no thought of a willingness to conserve.

On the north side of the square on the corner of Washington Street and facing south was Luke Lyle's Grocery Store. Next was the Georgia Power Company. Mr. Claude Y. Daniel was the manager. Next to the Power Company and occupying the rest of the block was Randolph's Funeral Parlor and Furniture Store. Later, prior to the destruction of the Harrison Hotel, Legg's Grocery Store moved to the corner that is presently a restaurant next to the Crawford Long Pharmacy. The pharmacy is owned and operated by Fred C. Gurley.

Just up the street from Pinson's Café was the Jefferson Ice and Coal Company owned and operated by Doss Wilhite and later was purchased by Mrs. Ethel Dadisman. They had large blocks of ice for home and commercial use and a customer could drive by and get any amount needed. They also made home deliveries. The worker at the plant wore a heavy rubber apron around his waist and with ice pick and tongs in hand was always ready to accommodate the customer. It is interesting to note that all of the ice was delivered to the icehouse by the Gainesville Midland Railroad. No ice was actually made there. Coal was available by the chunk, gunnysack or by the ton.

Next to the Icehouse was Carter's Bonded Warehouse, located at the junction of Elm and Randolph Street. They sold fertilizer, re-capped tires, and stored cotton. In 1959 Mrs. Ethel sold the icehouse and property to James and Vernon Carter and they continued to sell ice and coal behind their warehouse. The Carters also manufactured fertilizer in their plant located at the intersection of Hill and Elm Street. 4/ Just across the street from the fertilizer plant is the site of the old canning plant. Farther up Randolph Street was the Randolph Building that housed the Department of Agriculture and Dick Storey's Farm Tractor Parts Store. The Local Draft Board was upstairs and Ms. Helen Daily could have you serving your country with a quick stroke of the pen. Also upstairs was the Soil Conservation Office. Mr. Walter Carlan was the area Soil Conservationist. Next to the Randolph Building was Dad's business, The Planter's Bonded Warehouse. My father was a Cotton Broker and bought and stored cotton and sold fertilizer to the farmers. In his brokerage business Dad shipped cotton far and wide to many mills. Norman Brazeal was his truck driver for many years and when Brother Billy got his driver's license, he and I would deliver cotton samples for Dad. I remember going to Spartanburg, Greenville and Columbia, South Carolina on several trips. I also recall going to Boaz and Cullman, Alabama with Dad on several occasions.

I think it is interesting to note that in the prime cotton days there were many acres of cotton grown in Jackson and the surrounding counties. The figure of twenty seven thousand acres in Jackson County alone sticks in my mind during my high school days of 1946 through 1950. As young high school lads many of us worked the summer days as reporters, mapping the area farmer's cotton allotments on large aerial photographs framed in a plywood holder. The property lines were pre-drawn on the photos, identifying each farm throughout the county. Our job was to identify each field of cotton, give it a number and accurately measure and pencil dashed lines around it so it could later be measured in the office. Clerks using an instrument called the planimeter calculated the acreage, making sure the farmer stayed within their given allotment. By 1962 the cotton acreage in the county had dropped to about twenty five hundred acres.

The Randolph building burned just a few years ago and The Carter's Warehouse and The Planter's Warehouse have since been demolished. Now a parking lot occupies the total site, leaving only the old "Tater House" and Kinney's old seed cleaning facility lying between the Tater House and the old Depot as testimony to the days gone by.

Just up the street past the courthouse, Randolph Street intersected with Depot Street and just down Depot Street across from the depot was Charlie Daniel's Bar B Q place. Charlie was an African American gentleman and made the best hickory smoked Bar B Q in the county. You could always tell when he was cooking up a new batch by just sniffing the air.

In 1916, E. Scott Ethridge built a building for the purpose of curing sweet potatoes. It was a large concrete block building measuring fifty feet by a hundred feet. Spaced throughout the building were two feet by two feet holes in the floor covered with rabbit wire. Salamander heaters on the bottom floor were lit to provide heat to cure the potatoes. The heat rising up through the holes spread evenly throughout the building. The potatoes were delivered by local people and by the Gainesville Midland Railroad. There was a railroad spur directly in front of the building, making receiving and shipping of the potatoes very efficient. Hence the name "Tater House" was coined. 5,6/

In a few years Mr. Ethridge closed his potato business and renovated the upstairs of the building into apartments. There was a wide central hall with eight rooms on each side. The "Tater House," after the renovation was also known as the "Po Folks Home." Those were the days before public housing and many low-income families lived there. 5/

Mr. Ethridge had a concrete business and manufactured county boundary markers, curbing, cement blocks and concrete culverts. 6/ His factory was on the basement floor of the Tater House. In 1906 he attained patents on a very decorative cement block resembling a "granitoid" pattern. Stamped on the backside of each block was the inscription "Miracle Ho Lo Block' June 8,1908." 7/ The blocks were used in the construction of the Christian Church and the Ethridge-Daniel House. Some of the blocks were used in the trim work of Carter's Bonded Warehouse. 6/

Supplies for the concrete factory were delivered by the railroad. Cement ingredients were delivered through two 3 x 3 foot doors, one on each corner of the building. Water for the operation was pumped from a large spring. The spring was the source of Chrystal Branch that flows along the west boundary of the Ethridge-Staton-Gurley House.

In 1973 Mr. Ron Bond purchased the "Tater House" and the surrounding property for the purpose of establishing his business, Bonco Manufacturing Corporation and later Bonco Realty. Mr. Bond spent many days and weeks cleaning the grounds and renovating the building and is to be commended for leaving its appearance to commemorate its historical past. Most of the upper level is used for storage and his office occupies the northwest corner of the building. The basement was used for his chemical business of manufacturing water treatment chemicals. 4/

Mr. Bond pointed out that prior to the time he purchased the properties there was a short street running south from Elm Street along the western edge of the "Tater House" and connecting with Lee Street. The street was known as "Frog Alley." The alley has since been obliterated.

The Ethridge-Staton-Gurley House, reported to be the oldest house in the City of Jefferson, was built in 1836. 21/ It was owned by Mr. Ethridge in the early 1930s and was purchased by Jayne's parents in 1932. They lived there until 1941 when Mr. Staton sold the house to Mr. and Mrs. Fred C. Gurley. The Statons moved to Mr. E. E. Martin's house on Martin Street, site of the original Jackson County Academy School, and purchased it in 1945.

✕

Mr. Claude Catlett's Barbershop was a special place. It was located just up the hill next to Legg's Grocery Store. Legg's was on the corner of Washington and Lee Street, on the ground level of the southeast corner of the Harrison Hotel. As you entered the barbershop the red and white striped barber's pole was on the left and on the right was a large billboard that usually advertised Coca-Cola. The billboard also hid a vacant lot that was behind the hotel. Inside the barbershop was three chairs: Mr. Merk to the left, Mr. Catlett in the middle and Sam Doster to the right. Mr Merk chewed tobacco and would spit, with great accuracy I might add, into the nearby polished brass spittoon. He sure made chewing tobacco look good. Billy, C. B., Thomas and I tried to emulate his spitting technique but could never quite get it down pat. Never did know the not so lucky person who had the unpleasant task of cleaning and polishing those spittoons. On the wall was an Independent Life Insurance calendar with this quotation, "It is better to have it and not need it – than to need it and not have it." I have found that quotation to be applicable to many things other than life insurance. Later along with the Harrison Hotel, Legg's Grocery Store, the barbershop, the billboard and Mr. Whitehead's small Café were all demolished.

Growing up in Jefferson was a fun time, an adventurous time and a simple time, a time that just happened. We were born and everything was there waiting for us - our families, our friends young and old, our town and Lawrenceville Street. Everything that was needed for growing up, a complete menu plus many role models waiting their chance to help guide us through the early years. Up the street were the Lords, the Elrods and Ellingtons, the

Aderholts, the Leggs, Mr. Thompson, Uncle Morris and family, the Turners, the Culbersons and the Wills and next door were the Lyles and Doctor McDonald.

✕

I would be remiss if I failed to mention our African American friends on Lawrenceville Street. There was C. D. Kidd, Jr. and his family; Lite and Lonnie Callaway, their daughter Louise and her son L. W. and Bertha and Leroy. Ms. Lite, we called her, made some mighty fine biscuits and she would load them with real butter and you can well imagine why we all hung around when we smelled them cooking. She always welcomed us. C. D., III was about our age and we all hung out and played together. C. D. has really done well with his life. He has served as a City Councilman for many years and it makes me proud to have had him as a friend during those early years and now in our older years. Later my brother, John, came along and he and Elbert Kidd were very good buddies and they certainly left their tracks of mischief wherever they went. L.W. was a few years older but he was a good friend also. I remember Lonnie repairing chicken coops for the Lords and helping Mrs. Elrod with yard chores. Lite and Lonnie's house still stands in the alley behind the Elrod's and Lord's houses as a testimony to the days of old. C. D., Sr. worked for Dad for years and was a great friend to Billy, John and me.

✕

The square was a special place for both young and older folk. It was a place where people gathered to visit and was an especially fun place for dating couples to hang out. Even the city policeman on night patrol would stop by and visit. The stores on the north and south side of the square had apartments above them and the tenants would sit out on the balconies visiting with each other. The buildings on the south side have been renovated and the apartments are gone but those on the north side of the square are still there, balcony and all. At least one apartment is occupied to this day. The square was much larger in the early days having been reduced to the present day median in 1962 and that was done much to the displeasure of many folks.

✂

Farming was the way of life throughout Jackson County making Jefferson a true agriculture town. Saturday was always a special day, a day when the country folk would come to town to pay bills, buy supplies, shoe their horses, have their wagons repaired, bring their cotton for ginning at Fite's Gin or to peddle their home grown produce. Or maybe they would get a shave and haircut and just sit around visiting with friends. I can still hear the ring of the blacksmith's hammer as it struck the anvil and seeing the gents sitting around spitting tobacco and spinning tales. Rankin's Blacksmith Shop was located on the site that is now Seabolt's Small Engine Repair Shop. Mr. Singletary sold feed across from the blacksmith shop.

I remember one Saturday a farmer brought a heron or a great egret to town. He saw the heron down at his pond. It was cripple and unable to fly. Most likely it had a run in with an ole snapper turtle. The farmer tied the bird to a post at the blacksmith shop for everyone to see. There were a couple of hound dogs hanging out sleeping under a chinaberry tree and they took a keen interest in the bird. Now if you know anything at all about the 'heron family' you know it is best to leave them alone. That long beak was made for a purpose and the fact that it was attached to a long snake like neck made it a formidable weapon. But dogs get mighty brave when there are two or more and it became pretty obvious that these two idiot dogs had never seen anything quite like this crazy bird and they began their attack. One dog on each side of the bird and in a flash blood was streaming down both of the dog's faces. That bird struck both of them in a flash with deadly accuracy right on their heads, thus ending that confrontation. Those dogs got smart real quickly and went packing with their tails tucked between their legs.

I recall Mr. O'Dillon and Mr. Jet Roberts making regular visits through the neighborhoods delivering fresh vegetables, fresh butter and eggs, During the fall and winter days they delivered fresh sausage, lard, bacon and several meat products. Many deliveries were by special order. I remember the Dutch Oven Bakery truck stopping door to door selling baked goods and Mother buying salt risen bread and occasionally sweet buns for breakfast. The Standard Coffee truck made its regular rounds selling coffee and other goods.

Some homes had large lots that might qualify as mini-farms and many had large gardens, chickens, ducks and maybe a pig or two. Some even had barns, small pastures and milk cows. Mr. Phil Pendergrass lived on the edge of town in a very sparsely populated area and just a stones throw from our house. He rented the back of his lot to Mr. McMullen. Mr. Mac had cows and pigs on his place and had quite an enterprise going. On our street the Wills and Turners had pastures and barns with cows and chickens. The Langfords had a large garden. The Lords had a garden and many chickens. The Elrods had an onery heifer, "Old Red." That pasture belonged to her and she would put you up a tree in the wink of an eye. Mr. A. S. (Cap) Johnson owned the old Richardson House and lot that was probably one of the largest mini-farms in Jefferson. He had a tool shed, feed crib, a good size pasture and a "milk cow," plus a garden - everything a farm needed. Sidney even had a Shetlin pony at one time. The Johnson House is on Cooley Street, just across from the Methodist Church and was always a fun place to play. I shall never forget seeing their cow birthing a calf while we were sitting in the Home-Economics building during class. I don't know if we were supposed to watch or not but it sure caused an interruption for a good amount of time. Mrs. Castlelaw was beside herself and just did not know how to handle the situation. It had to be a first time event in school history.

My mother-in-law had chickens and a large garden and at one time managed to have two gardens. The Reverend Frank Barton, our Methodist Minister, lived next door to her and also had chickens. The Bartons visited us on several occasions at our summer home in Rabun Gap, Georgia. Each time they came up the Reverend would have a couple of hens in a coup tied to the front bumper. We would all sing, "she'll be coming round the mountain when she comes – we will kill the ole red rooster when she comes." Those fresh hens sure tasted fine made into chicken and dumplings.

Just imagine the kinfolk dropping in unexpectedly, usually just before dinner. The lady of the house would insist that they stay for dinner. She would rush out to the backyard and catch a chicken, wring its neck, put the chicken in a pot of boiling water and after removing the feathers and cleaning, the chicken was washed, cut into pieces, battered and ready for the frying pan. In a short while all would gather at the table and after saying "Grace," would enjoy the feast of their lives. Fresh fried chicken and gravy with green beans, tomatoes, onions, fried okra, mashed potatoes, biscuits and cornbread and ending with freshly made fried apple or peach pies and just maybe, a piece of homemade pound cake – all served with cold iced tea or fresh milk. That is the way it was growing up, spontaneous and just simply good.

Sometimes the leftovers from the days gone by seem to clash with the now. Our neighbors rent the property adjoining our back property line and ironically have rabbits, cats, dogs, roosters and hens. Somehow this just does not fit today's scheme of things.

That rooster can be heard crowing anytime, day or night. After they moved in it took some time for all of the adjoining neighbors to adjust to the new noise. I asked our minister if it was a sin to have murder of your neighbor's rooster in your heart. He replied, "Not if you are hungry." I did consider that to be an option for a short time but thought better of it. After all, the rooster is just doing what a rooster does and now we consider the situation as a part of the days of yesterday that simply will not go away.

****

Chapter Two

Before High School

Chapter two

IT WAS THE DAYS of the "Great Depression," and Mother and Dad had finished building their house in August 1930. The stock market crash of 1929 had left our country in a state of shock. Dad worked with the Jefferson Mill at the time, a time when it seemed to many folks that all hope to continue with their lives as they knew it was gone. The mill was the largest employer of people in Jefferson and as orders dried up, the wheels of the industrial business slowly came to a stop and the mill shut down in 1932. Mother and Dad had no choice but to leave Jefferson, having lived in their new home for just a few short months. They moved to Athens to live with our grandmother, Granny. Dad was able to rent the house to Colonel Henry Davis for the sum of twenty five dollars a month. Sister Frances was a big girl of six years and Brother Billy was two. I was born while we were living there. Our family moved back to Jefferson when I was almost a year old in 1933. 8/

The Lords moved to Lawrenceville Street in 1926, living first in the Culberson home and in 1935 moved into their permanent home between the Wills and the Elrods. The Aderholts built their house and moved from the Thompson house in 1935. The Lyles built their house next door to us about 1938, so the neighborhood was not quite complete until then.

The times had been marred by the depression, beginning in the late 1920s and lasting through most of the 1930s. World War Two began with Germany in 1939 and with Japan in 1941 and was finally over in 1945. This was a happy time and a sad time, but for us boys it was a great time to grow up. The war taught us many things about life. The most important lessons learned were: patriotism, sacrifice and that freedom is priceless. We were pretty much oblivious to the economic woes of the depression as we were all born during that time and that's just the way life was for us.

However, the experiences of our parents and others during those hard times had an everlasting effect on all of us. My mother and father-in-law, Mama Taton and Pop took advantage of every situation. Mama Taton was an excellent cook and would bake cakes and pies. Pop was working with the U.S. Department of Agriculture in Athens and would take the baked goods to work and sell them by the piece to his co-workers. Mama Taton was "frugal to a fault," as the saying goes and her motto was, "a penny saved is a penny earned." 2,9/ From experiences such as this we were taught frugality and sacrifice in every aspect of life. I remember hearing Mother say, "even a three cent postage stamp was hard to come by."

As soon as I came into the world, Billy and I became best friends and as time progressed he helped me to grow into the group. What Billy did I did and probably a hint of mischief was the day we walked to town with Emma Dee Burns. Emma Dee was our cook and housekeeper and as we strolled along we met Mr. L. B. Isbell outside of his grocery store on Washington Street. Mother did most of her shopping there. Mrs. Isbell was a very sweet and accommodating lady but Mr. Isbell could be quite grumpy at times. As we passed him Billy looked up and said, "damn fool" and not to be outdone, I looked back and said "damn fool." I was too young to remember but it is true, it happened. Despite Mr. Isbell's grumpy nature and reputation, according to Dad he got a good laugh out of the incident. Billy was about six years old. I wonder who put those carefully selected words in his head.

Billy; C. B. and Harry

C. B. and I were best friends and also bonded instantly. I do not know when it happened but as far as I was concerned he was part of the family and just another brother. We stayed together constantly and whatever he did I did and vice versa. Neither sickness nor injury could keep us apart. For example when he stepped on a broken bottle and cut his foot. It was a very serious cut requiring many stitches and for several days he was unable to ride his bike, but not to worry, I simply pulled him around in my red wagon until he was able to ride again. I don't think we missed a single Saturday movie at the Roosevelt Theater because of it. It was a terrible thing for a little one to mess up his summer vacation with an injury of any sorts because those out of school days were precious. But in the event it did happen, friendship could overcome most adversities or at least make them better. It was business as usual.

Even those days when C. B, Billy and Thomas were riding bikes, before I came of age to ride, I was able to keep up in most situations with my scooter, my push with one foot and coast scooter that is. I could keep up on short trips but had to ride on the cross bar for longer treks. But that did not last long because being big for my age, I was riding in no time. Bicycles were an important part of our lives and like all boys we tried to make them sound like cars. I remember C. B. had a classic model, like a luxury sedan. It had a push button horn and a built in light. Man, we thought that was the Cadillac of all bikes. I remember when we bought sirens, those little round things with a pull chain. It would clamp onto the frame and as you were whizzing along, usually at top speed, a pull on the chain would bring the post of the gizmo to rest against the turning wheel making the whirring sound that was supposed to sound like a siren. It worked and people really got out of the way when they heard us coming. The motors for our bikes was a deck of playing cards. Cards were fastened onto the wheel supports using wooden clothespins. Several cards, depending on how powerful a motor the individual wanted, were clamped onto the front wheel. The noise of the cards flapping the spokes sounded like a stiff stick being raked along a picket fence at a running speed.

Riding bikes could be a bit risky at times. For instance, a bad drive gear causing the chain to slip could cause an unwanted contact of the crotch with the bar. Now that stopped all actions immediately and it took a while for the victim to recover. Another action that could cause a pretty good wreck was getting your britches leg caught in the chain. When that happened, the rider was usually unable to operate the brakes. Bikes only had foot brakes back then and it was either coast to a stop or crash. Usually the crash came first.

As time progressed and we reached the upper elementary and early high school days our attention turned to football. As I recall those teams that received the most attention were Army, Navy and Notre Dame. C. B. was Navy all the way and Billy loved the Army team. Mine was Notre Dame because I liked their fight song and their green and gold school colors. Radio and newsreels highlighted the Army's Blanchard/Davis combo and the annual Army/Navy game. They were the most talked about. Georgia was just down the road but had not gained our loyalties at that time but I do remember going to the Georgia/Alabama game featuring Charlie Trippi and Harry Gilmer. Notre Dame always had a winning team and seemed to be hated by all.

There were no pee-wee sports leagues available for us back then, so learning the fundamentals of all sports was left to us. On most Sunday afternoons you would find us playing touch football in the vacant lot next to the Turners on Lawrenceville Street. We called it "Turner's Field." Kids from all over town would come over and challenge the kids on Lawrenceville Street. One group was very frustrated that they could never beat us. When the football season ended we turned our attention to basketball. We spent a lot of Sunday afternoons and later high school days playing in the old gym. We could always get in by simply lifting a corner of a sheet of tin and slipping in.

Baseball came much later and Billy and I would play pitch in the street in front of the house or throw the ball back and forth over the house. Brother John was born in 1946 and was fourteen years younger than me. The day Dad brought Mother and John home from the hospital, Billy, Willie Craig and I were throwing the baseball back and forth over the house. Billy was in the backyard and Willie and I were in the front yard. Billy let fly with the ball and Willie positioned himself under it and it smacked him in his right eye. Willie was wearing glasses and the ball crushed his glasses, severely cutting his face and eye, at almost the instant Mother and Dad drove up with Brother John. I got my bicycle and Willie got on the bar and away we went to Doctor Stovall's office. The Doctor fixed him up and assured him that his eye would be okay. Luckily it was okay and he had no further trouble with it.

Our grandmother's home was on the corner of Chase Street and Prince Avenue and the house was described as one of the beauty spots of Athens, "The City of Homes." We never knew our granddad, William Thomas Bryan, Sr. He passed away in 1922 at the young age of 55 years old but accomplished much during those short years. He was one of the organizers of the Athens Electric Railway System, being for a time its treasurer and then its president. 10/ He founded the Southern Manufacturing Company of Athens in 1902. That company became the largest concern of its kind in the United States. The company spun the refuse from cotton mills into a course cotton fabric used in the making of gloves and other rough cotton goods.11/ Granddad was one of the petitioners who purchased the Jefferson Cotton Mill out of receivership in 1916. Other petitioners were his younger brother Morris M. Bryan, Sr., Mr. J. Y. Carithers and Mr. John Tibbetts, all of Athens. 12/

Granny and Granddad married in 1895 and built their new home in 1913 and I think it is interesting to note how Granny happened to come to Athens and the consequences of her doing so. The following words were copied in part from the Athens Banner Herald.

"Doctor Edward Smith Lyndon was a prominent Athens pharmacist and businessman. However, few realized he was also a surgeon. After earning his medical degree, Dr. Lyndon went to Germany to further his medical studies. He was there when the War Between the States broke out and immediately returned home. He enlisted in the Confederate Army as a surgeon and was so affected by the horrors that he witnessed at the battle of the Crater at Petersburg, that he vowed never to practice medicine again.

"Dr. Lyndon came to Athens around 1880 and opened a drug store at the corner of Broad and Jackson streets. He was indirectly responsible for Dr. John 'Peete' Peebles Proctor, Granny's brother and co-founder of the St. Mary's Hospital, coming to Athens.

"Dr. Proctor's father (Dr. Thomas A. Proctor) was an old friend of Dr. Lyndon's in Virginia. He had lost touch with him during the war and after the war, wrote to him. Dr. Proctor wrote back, telling him that he had a daughter, Hattie, who was teaching school in Georgia. Lonesome for her own daughter who was away at finishing school, Mrs. Lyndon wrote Hattie to come to Athens for a visit. Hattie accepted and stayed six years. She ended up marrying William Thomas Bryan and making her home in Athens.

"The younger Doctor Proctor, after graduating from medical school, decided that since his sister was in Athens that he would settle here too. In 1907, with Dr. H. M. Fullilove, they founded and built St. Mary's Hospital." 22/

It is also interesting to point out that Dr. Thomas A. Proctor, a surgeon with the rank of Major served in the Army of Northern Virginia. He too, ceased practicing medicine because of the horrors he witnessed during the war. 23/

Dr. John Peeples Proctor died April 13, 1924 as the results of an automobile accident, which occurred as he was on his way to perform a surgical operation upon a patient at Jefferson that could not be delayed. 24/

Granny was born in Locust Grove, Virginia in 1865, the year the War Between the States ended. During her childhood her nanny was a former slave. Her name was Mammy and was dearly loved by all. Mammy had a daughter, Dora and after Mammy, along with the rest of the slaves had gained their freedom, they were given the choice to leave the plantation or become sharecroppers. Most agreed to stay. After Granny married, Mammy and Dora left the old home place and moved to Athens. Mammy continued her nanny duties, caring for my father when he was born and as a young lad. Dora was Granny's cook and housekeeper. We all loved Mammy and Dora and Dora seemed to have a special fondness for Billy. At least that's what Billy wanted me to believe. Each Sunday she would have a big box of sugar cookies waiting for him when we arrived. He would share a couple but claimed they were his.

Granny's health was beginning to fade in the late 1930s. During that time Mother and Dad, Frances, Billy and I would visit her on Sundays. Even though she was not well during our early years, she was a very strict disciplinarian. As I look back I realize now that she had every right to be a little ill tempered when we were all together. As time progressed it was necessary that Granny had to have a live-in nurse. Her name was Miss Graham. She was a real nice person and seemed to love children until I did a terrible thing. Our Uncle Joe, Mother's brother, gave Billy and me knives for Christmas. I was probably eight or nine years old at the time, much too young to have a knife. It was an official Boy Scout knife and the leather punch had a special appeal to me. Miss Graham kept her small leather suitcase under a cot in the upstairs bathroom. I drilled a hole in that suitcase and that was the impetus to learning one of the most important lessons of my life. Granny took charge, jerked a knot in my tail and proceeded with one of the greatest dressing downs of a human to this day. She taught me a mighty lesson in being respectful of others and their property, a lesson that I have never forgotten.

✂

Billy and I had some good times playing on those long paved driveways. Granny had a large lot. There was a greenhouse for growing everything needed to keep her flower garden beautiful and lush. George Flannigan was the groundskeeper and Granny's driver and seeing the movie, "Driving Miss Daisy," certainly brought back those memories. Also in the garden was an enormous scuppernong arbor. We had a great time playing under and even on top of it. Dad had a goat and a wagon when he was a boy. Usually the first thing Billy and I would do when we arrived at Granny's was to get the goat wagon out from the basement and pull each other around the grounds and coast down the driveways. We would also sit on the brick fence along

Prince Avenue and count the little Austin cars that would go by. The Austin seemed to be very popular in Athens, kind of like the Volkswagen Beetle of today. Entertainment was cheap in those days - you just did what was available.

On the way home on Sunday nights we would listen to Jack Benny or Edgar Burgen with Charlie McCarthy and Mortimer Snerd and we usually took the leftovers from dinner with us. Frances was not with us on this particular trip when we had baked goose for dinner. The goose was wrapped neatly and was on the back floorboard. Thinking Billy and I were asleep or quietly listening to the radio, Mother and Dad did not realize that we were eating the goose. When we got home, Mother could not believe her eyes. There was not an ounce of meat left on that carcass. Needless to say, Billy and I had no supper when we got home. We were full of goose.

In the winter of 1939, Billy, C. B. and I were nine and seven years old. We heard the weather report over the radio or maybe heard it from someone that snow was expected that night and would last through tomorrow. The light went on in our heads, "let's build a sled and get ready." We can make it out of the loose boards on the property line fence. Now, we guessed the fence was beginning to deteriorate to some degree and to use the boards would be okay. We proceeded to do that and when Dad came home, naturally he asked, "what are you boys doing?" We told him we were building a sled to use for tomorrow's snow. He laughed and said he hoped we were not disappointed if it did not snow. He said nothing about the fence boards so we figured that cleared us of any wrong doing there. But not to be discouraged by a few negative words, we continued with our project and after several hours of hard work it was finished. Our sled was completed and ready for storage under our bed. It weighed a ton but we finally got it stowed away. The next morning snow was several inches deep and still coming down. It was paradise in Jefferson, Georgia. We had never seen anything like it. After eating breakfast we rushed to get our sled and go outside. C. B. came down and when we put the sled on the ground it stuck like a fly sticking on fly-paper. It could wiggle but it was not going anywhere. It was a complete flop. But all was not lost as we quickly recovered from our failure and went over to Moore's Hill where the older boys were playing. They were sliding down and through the pasture to the creek on a sheet of old roofing tin, complete with its sharp corners and ragged edges. They let each of us slide down the hill a time or two and luckily no one was hurt. It was said that we had about nine inches, a record snowfall for the time that kept the school closed for several days and that was the best part of all. Boy, anytime you could beat the school out of a few days you were way ahead of the game and this was the jackpot.

Another time Billy and I decided we wanted a swimming pool in our backyard. That was a very uncommon thing to have back then because plastic products and such had not been discovered. Celluloid was the closest thing to plastic but was only used for special things like pocket- knife handles, fountain pen bodies, combs, brush handles and the likes. What does that have to do with a swimming pool? Well, first of all you do not just dig a hole in your backyard and fill it with water. Something is needed to keep the water in the hole and if we had a plastic liner or something to hold the water we would have been in business. We did not and instead wound up with a small empty hole lined with mushy mud. Why is it that to a child everything seems so simple?

From most of the failures that we faced as young boys, a lesson was learned. In this case something better was not far off. We already had our swimming pool, but not in our backyard. It was down in the school woods behind the Jimmy Bailey house, just across the branch in the young pine trees. A hole had been panned out, for its fill dirt I suppose, and it held water. It was a great place for us to swim. We called it "the pond." It was about two to three feet deep in the deepest part, including about six inches of mud. No one lived anywhere near and whenever we were there, off with the clothes and in we went. The water was always warm and about as muddy as the hole in our backyard but it was ours. Making do with what we had was a humbling experience.

⁂

Then there was the duck thing. Someone gave Dad a couple of ducks for Billy and me. Billy named his Goo-Goo! Mine unfortunately did not live long enough to have a name. Billy was giving both ducks a swimming lesson and mine mysteriously drowned. I think it swallowed too much water when Billy tried to make it swim under water. But anyway, Goo-Goo survived to be the meanest bird on Lawrenceville Street. He would attack anybody or any animal that even thought about setting its foot on his territory. He would lie in wait behind the shrubbery for any unsuspecting person to walk up the street. Then he would fly out and flog and peck its victim with relentless fury. I can still see Goo Goo at the top of the street after swimming in Aunt Mildred's fish pond. He would get in the middle of the road, spread his wings, take off and glide into our yard. He would do that every day. Mother was the only friend that Goo Goo had. She could make him or her, we never knew for sure, do whatever she wanted. He would never chase her but he sure gave Dad a merry chase. Goo Goo met his fate at the hands of "Luvie" who lived on Rat Row, now Gordon Street. She told Dad later that was the toughest bird she ever tried to eat.

Billy and I were very young when the ducks entered our lives but old enough to become set in some of our ways. One particular thing was when we awakened on Sunday morning and would go to the kitchen and make ketchup and sugar sandwiches.

30

We would get the comics from the paper, get back in bed, read the comics and eat the sandwich. Pretty crazy but this practice became a ritual, for a while anyway. When Goo Goo became a part of our lives we included him in the Sunday morning ritual until he got older and became onery and a little too noisy. Mother caught on and stepped in to end that little bit of fun.

Jayne also had a duck experience when she was very young. She and her parents were visiting with the Johnsons near Galillee on a Sunday afternoon. Jayne overheard her mother and Mrs. Johnson talking about ducks. Mrs. Johnson said that she had dressed several ducks and put them in the refrigerator. Jayne did not hear the rest of the story. When they left for home that evening Mrs. Johnson gave Jayne two ducklings to raise. During the course of the next few days the little ducklings disappeared. Mama Taton later discovered a shoebox in the refrigerator and when she opened it there were two little ducks, fully dressed and fully alert, proving that ducks are a lot of fun if you know how to use them. 2/

It was a late spring day and school was out. Dad was working and Mother was preoccupied with housework. Billy, C. B. and I were in the backyard, probably playing in the garage or on the roof. Garages were favorite places to play. They were completely separated from the house and all were special but ours was particularly special. Growing next to it was a large chinaberry tree about midway along the hidden side of the garage. It had a large branch about the same diameter as the main trunk growing along the side and up to the roof, kind of like an inverted elephant's snout. At the back end of the garage was an outhouse. Its roof was slightly lower than the eve of the garage. We could walk along the branch of the tree and step right off onto the roof of the garage and onto the outhouse. Because of the tree and the dense cover of privet bushes and vines, it was an excellent hiding place and a great place for smoking rabbit tobacco and corn silk in our little glass pipes and make plans for other things to do.

But today it was honeysuckle time. The sweet smell was everywhere and Billy or C. B. said, "let's make some honeysuckle candy." All the resources were there and the tools were tucked away somewhere in Mother's kitchen. If we were quiet she would never know and probably wouldn't care until it was too late. The vines growing on the property line fence had a bountiful supply of flowers that would provide the good taste of honeysuckle. We had pinched the base of many flowers and pulled the flower parts out to savor the micro drops of good sweet nectar. Shoot, with all of us working together we could have a pot full of nectar in no time. Well, not exactly. It did not work that way. After several hundred sacrificial flowers had been decapitated we might have accumulated a drop or two of the major ingredient, way short of being enough to fulfill our mission. There had to be a solution, but what? Ah – ha, the solution was there all along waiting in Mother's pantry – karo syrup! That's it, just what we need. Now we can use the entire flower and why wash them, they looked clean and anything that smelled that good had to be pure and edible. No more pinching and we were on our way. Just pour in the karo syrup, mix in the flowers, begin stirring and let nature take its course. After several minutes of stirring and tasting, several bent spoons stuck in the epoxy like mix and several ruined pots, all we got out of it was a stomach ache, the worst we ever had and we were yet to face the music. We had to face Mother. but being the saint she was, she assured us that death was not imminent. She pardoned us and we live today.

I do not know who claims the discovery of epoxy but I do know that a mixture of Japanese honeysuckle flowers and karo syrup comes pretty darn close and am pretty well convinced that the epoxy of today does indeed have those two ingredients in it.

I will have to say here that I was just a tag along being two years younger, not even old enough to be an apprentice but I was big for my age and could readily keep up. I did have a wagon so I was needed for this next venture. C. B. was the brain of the group, Billy was our public relations director and Thomas was our provider of supplies and other things. Survival is a strange thing and causes people to try and do about anything. Well, our survival was in the balance, we needed B-B bats and three cent colas, we called them three cent'rs. B-B bats were the suckers of the day, second only to the more expensive Brown Cow but a glass of water was essential for dipping and licking to fully enjoy the deep richness of the Brown Cow. That was much too cumbersome to be practical for busy boys. It was best to enjoy them while at home and besides it only came in caramel flavor. The B-B bat came in chocolate, vanilla, strawberry and banana flavors and we had to have them all. We were too young to have fillings in our teeth so we could really enjoy rolling them up in our mouths and chewing or simply letting them slowly melt. B-B bats were also good dipped in water but that was totally unnecessary and a waste of energy. Where in the world were we going to get the money to buy all these treats? We had tried the lemonade route. Every kid alive and those gone before us had tried that venture. There was no profit in lemonade. Our great opportunity lay just across the bridge in the school woods. The school woods was the property of Martin Institute and lay adjoining the school to the north and to the east. It was filled with large trees, had a log cabin, a few gullies, vines to swing on and a branch running through its entire length. The woods were a perfect setting for growing up boys. It could be and was anything we imagined it to be. It was our land of opportunity, a place to explore and grow.

The branch divided the woods into two parts, the south part with the big trees, shrubs and vines. The north part was several acres of young pines planted at the turn of the decade and now dotted with several homes. The pines were in their infancy and the road was lined with wild plum and blackberry bushes. The idea, "let's get our wagons and pick blackberries and plums and sell them to all of our neighbors." Everybody likes fruit and berries. There is absolutely no way this can fail. It sounded like a good idea and with unanimous approval we set about planning our next move. We were going to be so rich we could buy all the B-B bats Mr. Baxter had in his store. Why had we not thought of this before?

Somehow things just do not work out as planned. Our first obstacle was the plums were ripe for picking but the blackberries were waning. So due to the uncooperative nature of the season, we had to settle with just plums. Oh well, everybody loves plums and we began filling our wagons. The road was unpaved and not very well maintained. It went to the old track field that was used for the high school sporting events and many other uses such as target practice, Boy Scout outings, kite flying and just messing around - a lot of messing around I might add. The road serviced only two families and looped back into highway 129.

We gleaned and cleaned the plums as best as we could and proceeded to canvas the neighborhood. Knocking on every door and being rejected at each was just not the way things were supposed to go. Mother and Mrs. Lord were the only ones to buy our goods either out of pity or to reward us for our hard work. We had a lot of good plums to dispose of and eating many during harvest and delivery we wound up with the worst case of intestinal upheavals any boys ever had. We had a more descriptive term for that condition but I will spare the reader the details. Man, it lasted at least two days and its effects lingered on for several more days. That was the end of the plum business and for plums in general. Heck, we might as well have tried lemonade again. Dad and Doctor Lord got a real laugh out of our experience but Mother and Mrs. Lord could only feel loving pity for us.

In 1936 or 1937 when I was very young, Mother, Billy and I were taking our dog Bozo to the veterinarian in Athens. The road was unpaved but well maintained as I suppose all of the main highways were back then. We were in Oconee Heights, just north of the Saint James Baptist Church when I decided I wanted to be up front with Mother. I opened the back door and the next thing I knew I was bloody and screaming as I lay in the ditch. Doors opened backwards on the cars back then and that caused my quick ejection from the car. A colored gentleman, a true Good Samaritan, saw me fall and immediately picked me up from the ditch and carried me over to the well house at the church. Billy told Mother that I had fallen from the car and Mother was beside herself, as you can well imagine. The gentleman was washing the grit and dirt from my wounds the best he could when Mother got there and he assured her that I was okay. We returned to Jefferson and to Doctor Lord's office as quickly as possible. Doctor Lord and Nancy finished cleaning my wounds and used a tremendous amount of mercurochrome. I was scratched and bruised from head to toe but Doctor Lord with his joking and gentle manner could fix a little boy any day. Bozo had to wait to see his doctor. But that was okay, he did not want to see him anyway.

****

Chapter Three

Saturdays-Movies-Make Believe and Messing Around

Chapter three

Saturday nights were special in the growing up days, before the war and for a few years after. On summer evenings many families would go down to the drug store and just socialize. The gents would gather in their respective groups and proceed to solve the problems of the times. The ladies would join each other and discuss whatever ladies discussed in those times. It was all a time of family and neighborly togetherness. The young folks played games on the square, such as tag you are it, or just hung out. There was hardly any traffic to contend with and the parents were not the least bit concerned about safety because everybody pretty much took care of each other.

There was a time during those years that Mr. O.L.Singletary had a bowling alley over on Athens hill between what is now the Mexican Restaurant and the Jefferson Tire Company. Mother and Dad would take us over there on the hot and humid summer nights. The men would bowl and the ladies just sat around visiting with each other. We watched as the men perspired profusely and drank Coca Colas at a steady pace as they bowled, talking, laughing and having a good time. On other occasions I remember going to Mr. McCree's house on Athens Street and playing while the ladies sat around visiting each other and the gents played croquet on the lawn. Those were some well spent moments, insignificant at the time but created many wholesome memories. Jayne also remembers those nights at the McCree's. We probably played together at times never suspecting that we would later marry and spend the rest of our lives together.

We spoke or waved to everyone who passed by during those days and it seemed we knew almost everyone. We were one big happy family but today everybody is in such a hurry we seem to have lost that feeling of togetherness. Even though we are still a small town, we are spread over all creation and often do not even know our neighbors. But I digress as I yearn for the days of long ago.

✂

Mr. Willie Colquitt was a farmer and peach grower in the Apple Valley community and Dad and Mother would take us to their orchard and packing shed to purchase fresh peaches. On occasion we picked them straight from the tree. There was nothing like eating a fresh peach, fuzz and all while standing in the shade of the tree amongst the buzzing June bugs. There were several peach orchards in and around Apple Valley but no apple orchards. I never quite understood why it was called Apple Valley when it was all peaches until recently. Apple Valley was named for many apple orchards established there at the turn of the century by Judge W. J. Colquitt of Athens, Georgia. It is said that the apple orchards were completely destroyed by a plague in the 1920s and were replaced with peach orchards.13/ Other orchards in the community were the Wilson's Orchard and Hawkin's Orchard that later became Booth's Orchard. I believe the Booth Orchard was the last to close.

On one particular Saturday evening Mr. Willie Colquitt brought his monkey to town. His name was Jab-bo. Old Jab-bo was wise way beyond his years. Jab-bo was not very big but was quick as a flash of lightning and very noisy and had absolutely no sense of humor. He jabbered all the time. That may be how he got his name. Jab-bo drew a pretty good crowd, including every age group of men, women and children alike. Mr. Colquitt brought along a poke of peanuts to reward Jab-bo when he performed properly. Mr. Bob Johnson was there and he was chewing gum. Now old Jab-bo took a great interest in the fact that Mr. Johnson seemed to really enjoy that gum and even though he did not know what he was chewing, he wanted some. He was on top of someone's car and began to edge closer and closer. Mr. Johnson handed a piece of gum that was still in the wrapper to Jab-bo. He took it, slipped off the outer wrap, unfolded the tinfoil and proceeded to chew the gum just the way Mr. Johnson did. In the meantime Mr. Johnson put another piece of gum in his mouth and kept the wrapper, folded it and put it back like a fresh piece of gum. In a few minutes he said, "hey Jab-bo, do you want another piece of gum?" Jab-bo gave a monkey yes, rushed over took the gum and began to unwrap it. He opened the tinfoil and found nothing there. Without hesitation he reached out, slapped Mr. Johnson in the face, knocking his glasses and hat off and headed for places unknown. He was gone in the wink of an eye. Everyone except Mr. Johnson went looking for Jab-bo. The great monkey chase was on. Jab-bo was found in Mr. Y. D. Maddox's old barn that was on the site where the present Region's Drive In Bank is located. There was no way Jab-bo was coming down from those high rafters. Heck, it looked for a while like the barn was going to be his new home but he finally got over the humiliation of the event and after a couple of hours came down for Mr. Colquit. I guess he figured he best not end his relationship with the hand that fed him, the hand that he could trust. The moral of that story, at least for Mr. Johnson was, "don't monkey around with another man's monkey." A good lesson for us all.

Saturday nights were always Sunday School and Church preparation nights. First we had to have the proverbial Saturday night bath. After the bath the shoes had to be cleaned. The shoe usually got more attention than the body it belonged to. We only had one pair, unlike the kids of today who might have several pairs. Just by pure fact alone that one pair looked pretty rough by weeks end, requiring not only polish but a thorough cleaning with a rag and sometimes a bit of shoe dye for the scrapes. Then came the polish and brushing and rubbing process until they passed the eye of the inspector. By the time I entered the army I was pretty well trained in shoe upkeep. Conservation was a way of life and we did not even know it.

Saturday was movie time at the Roosevelt Theater. It was cowboy, Indian, stagecoach and bank robbing time in the old west days. Several hours of each Saturday were spent watching the newsreels, the short serials, the Pete Smith Specialties, cartoons and the movies. We would go to the movie about eleven o'clock and come out about two o'clock, leaving a good part of the day for playing and spending some time at Joe Baxter's General Store. We would go there and read his comic books located at the front of his store. We sat on the floor and read the books and drank three cent colas. That was enough to satisfy Mr. Baxter or pay our way, so to speak.

The movies would start with the short newsreel, next the cartoons or Pete Smith Specialties, the Serial and then the main feature. The newsreel was an especially important part of the movie day, especially during World War Two. More about that later. The Serials would end with "continued next week." That was done to entice us back for next Saturday but was totally unnecessary because we were sure to go back anyway. It was the thing we boys did on Saturday. The serials featured Buck Rogers, Flash Gordon, the Shadow-"who knows what lurks in the heart of man? – "the Shadow do" and Clyde Beatty the animal trainer and many others. The specialties usually featured Laurel and Hardy, Abbott and Costello. Buster Keaton, Edgar Kennedy, Leon Erroll, The Three Stooges, Captain Marvel, Superman, Green Hornet, Our Gang and Bat Man. The Cartoons were Popeye, Looney Tunes, Bugs Bunny, Speedy Gonzales - the fastest mouse in the west and others. The main features were always thrillers, featuring Gene Autry, Tex Ritter, Lash Larue, Roy and Dale Rogers with the Sons of the Pioneers and their sidekicks – Gabby Hayes and Frog, Buck Jones, Tim McCoy, Hoot Gibson, Red Ryder and Little Beaver, Hopalong-Cassidy, The Lone Ranger and Tonto, Tarzan, and Zoro. Whoever we saw at the movie was who we became.

Now, to become what you saw at the movies was a process in itself. We never pretended to be anything, no way. "We made believe." To say let's pretend got us nowhere but when we said, "let's make believe," now those words had power and transported us to a different world far removed from where we were at the time. A whole new dimension was born.

✕

Usually after the movie if we did not go to Baxter's store, we headed for the school woods and made believe but we never made believe to be Clyde Beatty. He looked pretty silly, always carrying a chair and a whip and wearing those up to the knee laced boots, tools for wild animal tamers I guess, but he never changed. To carry chairs around would be a bit awkward for four boys. It wouldn't look right either. One day we were making believe we were super heros. We were in our side yard and Billy had a towel pinned around his neck, he was Captain Marvel. He was up about four feet off the ground in a privet bush and yelled out, "Shazam!" Shazam was the magic word that caused a lightning bolt and a clap of thunder that immediately changed the other guy into Captain Marvel, the super hero. Well, Billy shouted that magic word and leaped from the bush, hung his cape on a snag, hit the ground and broke his arm. That took him out of action for a few weeks, in fact for the rest of the summer. Other times we made believe we were Zoro and would ride our make believe stick or cane horses, waving our wooden swords in the air and singing Zoro's theme song, - "We ride with the wind as we go side by side, Zora's legion far and wide." We would have sword fights and they would get pretty rowdy at times. On one particular occasion we all had our smallpox immunization and the scabs had formed. We were told to protect that scab at all cost. There was to be no swimming at all and absolutely no messing around. Messing around pretty much covered everything. But we were messing around anyway. Thomas had a really big scab and as we were fencing and slashing with our stick swords someone sliced that scab right off of his arm. Bleeding profusely he lit out for home. He later got a fancy plastic guard to protect his wound. We all wanted one after that.

$$\propto$$

The escapades of Robin Hood gave us a few ideas too. Seeing Robin Hood and Little John and his gang sitting around the fire pit, roasting a pig or some other critter seemed to appeal to us. Going to the woods one day with our Red Ryder air rifles, we saw a mourning dove sitting in a small tree. We shot it and I can't remember who it was but someone said, "Let's cook it." That sounded like a good idea but you don't just cook something, it has to be prepared. I was the chosen one to run back home and get some margarine and salt and pepper. When I got back the bird had been picked and cleaned and ready to cook. We built a fire just like Robin Hood would do, made a spit, plastered the bird with margarine, salt and pepper and placed it over the fire. After several minutes over the fire the bird was deemed to be ready. Raw dove is not too good. Maybe a pig would have been better!

The Red Ryder air gun was not just a gun. To us it was a repeating Winchester, "the gun that tamed the West and Jefferson too." Another weapon we had to have was the bow and arrow. The bow and arrow were special things for sure and there was a special way to make them. Britt Elrod was our older neighbor and showed us how. He was certainly my mentor and his influence helped lead me to become a forester. First you need a three foot young hickory sapling, freshly cut and about an inch and a half in diameter. Trim it clean of all knots and bend and wedge it between the studs of a garage or barn. We preferred the Will's barn because it was out of the way and there would be no one to ask questions. After the stick had dried for a couple of weeks, add the string and you had a bow. The arrows were fairly easy to make. All that was needed was a good straight stick or cane. The joints on cane were a little rough and took a lot of time to smooth down. We preferred the stick. Cardboard or most anything rigid made a good quill but the point was special. A Coca-Cola or Pepsi-Cola bottle cap made an excellent arrowhead. Simply remove the cork from the cap, bend the cap around the big end of the stick, tap it tight and it was complete and ready for attacking the cowboys. (Sadly, Britt passed away less than two months after Jayne and I retired and returned home. He is sorely missed.)

Usually the cowboys and wagon trains would rest along their journey west at Steven's Rocks. The Rocks were over on what is now Elder Drive near the intersection of Dixon Drive, and consist of large boulders and trees scattered over an acre or so. It was excellent cover for camping and very secure against Indian attacks. Many Indian and Cowboy shootouts took place there. But other things happened at the Rocks, one in particular that we would like to forget. The Rocks were about a mile from our homes. At this particular time in our lives there were no paved roads so we usually walked rather than ride our bikes when we went there to play. Dixon Drive was the only road and it was not maintained very well past Ms. Ella Dixon's home. From there the road went through woodlands to the Steven's home and farm and made a sharp turn to the left. In that turn on the left side was a watermelon patch. Just a little farther on was a tenant house in plain view of the melon patch but if we were careful we would not be seen.

Watermelons were everywhere, big ones, little ones and the temptation was just too much. We thumped the melons until we about wore out our thumpers and never found a ripe one but there was another way. We had our knives and started plugging those melons. If the melon was not ripe we simply put the plug back in the hole thinking nobody would ever know. Well, all of a sudden there was a voice that yelled out, "C. B. Lord, Billy and Harry Bryan! You boys get out of that watermelon patch!" It was Roosevelt Grissom, he lived in the tenant house and was farming that ground for Mr. Love Whitehead who either leased the land from Mr. Stevens or owned it outright. We did not know who owned it but what we did know was, we were not careful enough and were in deep, serious trouble. We were caught for dead sure destroying those watermelons just as effectively as a bunch of crows, and people shoot crows. We figured our punishment would justifiably be the same. We shot out of there and ran the full mile home. We were eating supper that evening and there was a knock on the door. Dad answered the door and said, "hello Love, what brings you by the house." When Billy and I heard who it was and what it was about we shot out from there and hid under the bed. Mr. Whitehead left and we knew our moment of reckoning was there. Dad gave us a couple of good licks, took our knives away, cut off our ten cent weekly allowance and grounded us for two weeks, beginning at that moment. There was to be no bike riding whatsoever. Those two weeks were mighty slow in passing. C. B. got a good reprimand but was not grounded. He was able to taunt Billy and me a little bit by riding down and blowing his bike horn. For me this was a continuation of the suitcase episode with Granny. The lesson I learned there was temporarily forgotten but was never to be forgotten again. Respect for others and their property is a must and would never be violated again, under any circumstances.

The school woods Log Cabin was used for many things and events over the years. It is now owned by the Bells and is their home. It has a pretty long history, probably built around 1900 or so and was a part of Martin Institute. The cabin's uses were varied for most of the years we knew it until after the school burned in 1942. At that time it became the sixth grade and the first sex education class in our school system was taught there. The teacher took it upon herself to educate the girls and boys about the birds and bees. The boys would go outside when the girls were being taught and sneak under the cabin and listen. I always figured the girls did likewise when the boys were being instructed as to the ways of the birds and bees. Some of the girls who were in that class said they did not but we who know say, did too! I personally did not have the pleasure to be in that class and our teacher did not enlighten us on the subject. Our sixth grade was taught in the Home Economic building.

The cabin was our Boy Scout Lodge for a time, Troop Number 65, the Screaming Eagles met there. Clyde Boggs and Britt Elrod were our Scoutmasters and were assisted by Mr. Carlyle. The cabin was also the meeting place of "The Sons of the Rajahs." The Rajahs was an exclusive boy's club that never did anything good but never did anything bad. Their biggest event was the annual wildlife stew. I joined a couple years after Billy and C. B. and went through the initiation and participated in a couple of their wild game feast. Totsy Wilbanks was the stew master and it was always pretty good or at least we said it was. We knew better than to make the cook mad. The club members would go out the day before the stew, with guns in hand and bag anything they could. The usual ingredients were squirrel, rabbits, doves, quail and don't ask. We would all take part in dressing the game and Totsy cooked the stew in a large caldron. He always added enough red pepper to make it good and spicy, sometimes too spicy.

The Club's initiation was pretty bad. The members shaved the private parts of the inductee and smeared on a concoction of ketchup, salt and pepper and tied a string to the dangling part, which was a mite uncomfortable to say the least. The string was routed over the shoulder and appeared on the backside. A tag was tied to the end of the string saying, "please pull." Now, there was a lot of good acting done the next day at school. Whenever there was a jerk who gave a jerk on the string the inductee hollered out in agonizing pain but naturally the string was tied to the belt or elsewhere. If he was smart, that is.

Just messing around was another use of the cabin and probably was the most frequent use. For instance, "the pooting contest." The names are withheld for the sake of secrecy and to preserve the integrity of those involved, as this event has never been aired to the public. The cabin had window seats on three sides. The contestants would move about any way they wished and judged each other. One contestant could get on all fours and – 'put-put-put-put' - sounding like a one cylinder John Deere tractor. He could put-put anytime he wished and for as long as he wished. Really, there was no competition there. It was a complete 'blowout.'

Another favorite place on summer evenings was the Riverside Swimming Pool located on the Winder Highway just across the Middle Oconee River Bridge. The pool was owned and operated by Mr. Jim and Ms. Mattie Bell. Mr Bell was Jefferson's Chief of Police at the time. Ms. Mattie and their daughter Tommie pretty much ran the place but Chief Bell was often around. They also had a drive-in restaurant. The pool was filled from an artesian spring and the water was as cold as an Artic breeze. I remember the "spring peepers," singing in the swamp and along the river banks and hearing the brrr-rump, brrr rump of the jumbo bullfrogs echoing throughout the nearby swamp. Breathing the clean air and smelling its freshness are all time honored priceless memories. There was always a big happy crowd at the pool, kids of all ages and grownups too. Mr. Jim and Ms. Mattie were very sociable and congenial people and would usually spend equal time chatting with everyone. Chief Bell and Dad were good friends and enjoyed visiting with each other. Mother and the ladies talked and laughed and had a good time. Dad challenged us one night. He said he would give fifty cents to the first one of us who learned to swim. C. B. won the prize but we were all swimming pretty soon afterwards. The old pool was abandoned a few years later after the Bells could no longer manage it but Horace Singletary either leased or purchased the restaurant and managed it for several more years. Horace also managed the Joy Soda Shop for several years. Both places were very popular, especially for dating couples. In the early 1950s the Jefferson Mill began the Day Camp program and cleaned out or renovated the old swimming pool on the Old Swimming Pool Road. The pool remained open for a few short years and closed when the pool on Memorial Drive was completed and opened in the middle to late 1950s. Remnants of the old Riverside Pool are still there giving those who remember a chance to relive the wonderful bygone years.

Chapter Four

Swimming-Anytime-Anywhere

Chapter four

OF THE MANY THINGS we did during the summer months, swimming was probably by far the most important. Water is the sustenance of life but to growing boys it is even more than that. Life ain't worth a plugged nickel if there is not a pool or stream to jump into. That's a God given fact and we were running out of swimming holes. Billy and I had tried the back yard swimming hole venture. We had outgrown the school woods pond and the Riverside pool was just too far away. Riverside was definitely not a spur of the minute swimming place because Moms and Dads were not available on a spur of the minute call. We still had Curry Creek down at the White Bridge. Some people want to call it the Curry Creek Bridge but it just ain't so. Call it what it is, the White Bridge.

Curry Creek was okay but was much too shallow in most places, except where it made a turn and undercut the bank. It had not been dredged for flood control at the time and usually along the outside bank there would be a deep hole. That was the case under the bridge. There was a great hole along the bank and along one of the bridge pillows. It was not very wide but it was long and deep and we spent some good times there but it just was not sufficient. We needed a good swimming hole that was readily accessible and large enough for jumping and diving into.

It happened like a gift from heaven. We were playing at the McMullen house on the corner of College and Institute Street. Mr. Mac was working in the yard and we urged Thomas to ask him to take us swimming out at Riverside. Mr. Mac, sounding a little agitated said, "why don't you boys dam up the school woods branch and make yourselves a swimming hole?" "How, we asked?" "Use sand bags," he said. "Okay, by golly we will," we said but where could we find enough bags for this project?

We began to think and our first thoughts were flour sacks. Old flour sacks were very important to the ladies in the old days for making aprons, dish towels and other items. We thought they might be too small and flimsy for our use. Our needs were something much larger and stronger, like feed sacks. Mr. Singletary came to mind, he sold feed for livestock and feed came in croaker or gunnysacks. Maybe he would let us have his old ones. We went down to his place to talk to him. Mr. Singletary was a large man, not fat – just big and he always had a stub of a cigar in his mouth. He walked with a cane and leaned on it when he stood around talking. We asked him if he had any feed sacks we could have and I remember his reaction. He threw his head back laughing and said, "what in the world do you boys want with dirty old feed bags?" We told him our plan to build a dam on the branch so we could have a place to swim. I guess he thought that was an industrious thing for boys to do and said, "see that stack of old bags in the corner over there, you boys just help yourselves. I was going to have them burned pretty soon." We rescued several dozen from the fiery furnace and carried them to Thomas's house.

We then went down to the branch to find a place to build our pond. The perfect place was down the alley between the Frank Holder house which is presently owned by Ron Bond and the Phil Pendergrass house - presently the A. G. Mitchell house, at the lower end of the pasture. There was a small bluff created where the creek undercut the bank underneath the large sweet gum trees. It was a shady spot and there was a large sandbar giving us plenty of sand to fill our bags. Now if our calculations were right this pond would be big enough to do some serious swimming. Everything was falling into place. We had our dam site, our tools, supplies and resources, now it was time to go to work. We began to sort through the sacks and found many had large tears and rips in them and some were useless. We figured that was why Mr. Singletary laughed when we asked for the sacks. But that was okay. We sorted out the best for the foundation and resorted to repair the others using wire to stitch them up. Wire did not work too well. We found string to be much better.

Now that the problem was solved we began laying the foundation. Everything was going along pretty good until we began the second level of sacks. Each sack was laid in place and as the water was rising leaks began to appear. The sacks did not seal completely. We tried to correct the situation by packing wet mud in each joint but wet mud that stays wet does not seal. Another lesson in life was about to be learned.

As we were eating supper that night Dad asked how our dam project was coming along. We told him pretty good but we could not seal the joints where the sacks joined. We told him about the mud. He suggested that we use cotton to seal the joints and to bring several bags down to his office in the morning and fill them with cotton. Dad left the Jefferson Mill in September 1944 and began his own cotton brokerage business. He had all the cotton we needed and told us to wet the cotton and pack wads of it into the holes. We filled the empty sacks and headed back to the dam site. We did as he had told us and it worked like a charm. Lesson learned – when your back is against the wall, go to the expert.

We soon had the best dam in the country. In fact, we had more water than we ever imagined. However there was one thing we overlooked. In our haste to get started building our dam, we had not cleared the alder bushes along the bank and ended up hacking them down as best we could. We ended up with a whole lot of sharp stumps sticking out of and just beneath the surface of the water. We had to stay clear of that side of our pool because someone would surely get hurt.

We were swimming one day and Thomas was not with us but came down later. He said, "look what I found this morning." He had a nice looking silver ring. It looked like a ladies ring and we asked what he was going to do with it. He said he did not know but later one of us suggested that we bury the ring on site and call this place, "Treasure Island." Thomas agreed and the legacy of Treasure Island lives on today. We never knew where Thomas found the ring.

We were proud of our accomplishment. So proud in fact, that we invited our parents to come down and see it. I remember Mother and Dad coming and they could hardly believe that we could start and complete such a project. But our problems were not over. On a Sunday afternoon we went down for a swim. It had rained pretty hard on Saturday night. When we got to the pond it was a total washout. We could not believe our eyes, all that hard work and it's all gone. But not to be outdone, we built it back stronger than ever and did not have that problem again. We enjoyed Treasure Island for a couple of years. It was truly a great time in our lives and a great lesson learned. "If you really want something in life, work hard and you can have it."

Jefferson has three major streams running through the area, the North Oconee River, the Middle Oconee River and the Mulberry River. The North Oconee is just east of Apple Valley. The Middle Oconee flows by Riverside just west of Jefferson and the Mulberry is the boundary of Jackson and Barrow counties. We heard of a good swimming hole on the Mulberry, at the double bridges on the Double Bridge Road, which is an extension of the Ethridge Road. Many good and a couple of bad times were spent swimming and playing there. We were not driving at the time. It would be a couple more years before we were able to do that, so we had to have someone older to go out there with us. E. A. and

B.K. were probably sixteen or seventeen years old and took us on several occasions. The roads were all dirt and rutty and certainly were not the best for driving on but E. A. would let us ride on the fenders. One on each side holding onto the hood ornament and straddling those big headlights on Dad's Chevy. We would do this each time we went there until the day someone saw us and told Dad what we were doing. Dad put an immediate stop to our stupidity and threatened to take our swimming rights away unless we promised to cease that foolishness. Needless to say, we did! As best as I can remember that was E. A's last time to take us.

After that Britt Elrod and Mr. Carlyle took us out there on several occasions. Mr. Carlyle was with us the time we had the great mud battle. There was a rope hanging from a large birch tree leaning out over the river and it would give you a long wide swing around and to the middle of the river. We decided to have a free for all mud battle. There were no rules, everyone against each other trying to get control of the rope. I had it and was swinging out and almost ready to turn loose when Billy let fly with a mud ball and it hit me in the right eye. Man that hurt, my eye was wide open and it was packed with mud. Luckily there was not a rock in it. Mr. Carlyle came to my rescue and did the best he could do without doing further damage. He removed most of the mud from my face but having only river water he did not try to remove any from my eye. The Ethridge Farm was just a short distance down the road and Ms. Joyce took charge. She used fresh well water and flushed my eye several times and put a clean cloth over it until I could get to the doctor. When we arrived at Doctor Lord's office I still could not see. Doctor Lord rolled my eyelid back and said, "young man, there must be a ton of grit in your eye but we can get it out." After several more visits Doctor Lord said my eye had several scratches but otherwise looked good and would be okay. Doctor Lord could fix anything. We played and swam at the Double Bridge swim hole for several years creating many memories of some great times.

During our Boy Scout days we would hike about five miles to Hurricane Shoals to camp and earn merit badges. The Shoals did not have a very good reputation in those days and sometimes some pretty rough people hung out there. The local people would drive their cars out onto the shoals and wash them, using buckets for rinsing the soap. We would swim in the potholes and at the bottom of the shoals being careful of broken glass, etc. The Shoals were a lot of fun and we spent most of the time wearing out our butts on the slick rocks.

Other places we swam were the Commerce City Pool and the Gainesville City Pool. We would ride our bikes to Commerce but would take the bus to Gainesville and hitch hike from the bus station to the City pool. On many weekends, during our early college days several of us would go swimming in the Stegman Hall swimming pool at the University of Georgia. We also swam in the Athens City pool and many hours of fun were spent there.

∝⃝

Many fun days were spent at Lake Rabun and Lake Burton, in the early years and later during our dating days. Lake Rabun was the most popular during the 30s, 40s and through the 1950s. Lake Burton was pretty much a wilderness lake with just a few shacks or cabins dotting its shoreline. We could rent a wooden flat bottom boat with a five horse power motor for seven dollars a day from LaPrades Boat Dock and put-put around the lake. We would jump over the side and swim at a whim and later fish, hoping to catch the big one. Catching the big one never happened but the times spent there have never been forgotten. Jayne and I have a small cabin near the lake and have relived some of those days and love the tranquillity of the surrounding mountains. The lake and shoreline has now become very much over crowded and has lost a lot of its wilderness appeal, at least as far as I am concerned, but the younger generation have their speedboats and jet skis and the crowds seem to thrill them.

✕

Lake Rabun, on the other hand, seems to have become stable insofar as new construction and overcrowding is concerned and is pretty much like it was in the old days. There are a lot of new owners and a lot of tearing down and rebuilding on the old sites but basically it is pretty much the same. Hall's Boat Dock was the only place of entertainment on the lake for our generation and those before us and some mighty good times were had there.

In 1948 C. B., Paul Ferguson, Junior Lloyd and I rented a cabin at Halls. We had a great and exciting time fishing, swimming, hanging out at the boat dock and later helping Guy Hall. It rained excessively over the weekend, never ceasing torrential rains causing flash flooding in some areas and the lake to rise rapidly. The floodgates on the dam were wide open but could not handle the deluge of water pouring from the sky. Guy called on us for help. We went out on the lake with him in his Chris Craft, probably the most powerful boats on the lake for those times, to help raise the private boats out of harms way. If they were not raised many could break loose and be lost down the river. We figured that we saved many boats that day. On one occasion as we neared the dam the current was so swift from the tremendous flow of water thundering through the floodgates, we feared we might be swept down river. Guy turned the Chris Craft into the current and at full throttle slowly pulled us free. What an experience!

All the roads leading to the lake were flooded and that gave us an extra day or two at the lake. Doctor Lord was later able to pick us up and took us home. That was one of those unforgettable experiences.

On another occasion C. B., Billy, Willie Craig, Stan Escoe and I went camping at the campground near Rabun Beach. We rented a flat bottom wood boat, powered by the usual five horse Johnson motor and docked it at the beach. We used the boat for swimming, fishing and messing around. The campsite was in the National Forest and was primitive as all were in those days. We had no tent and no sleeping bags, just blankets and the ground, of course there was very little sleeping anyway. We sat around the campfire and Stan entertained us by imitating a Scottish bagpipe. He would hold his nose and tap his Adam's apple with the edge of his hand and give a darn good rendition of a Scottish tune. Stan was quite a fellow. He was a few years older than we were and was a great guy. He passed away not too many years after that camping experience.

When the time came to go home, C. B. and I were chosen to take the boat back. It was about two miles and would probably take about an hour and a half to get back to Hall's, if all went well. Old 'Sol' was bearing down and after a few minutes chugging down the lake we decided it was time for a cooling swim. We shut the motor down and jumped into the lake and after several minutes we climbed back into the boat. We wrapped the crank cord around the flywheel and pulled, it did not start and after a dozen pulls we were about worn out. That darn motor just up and died. We had a couple of paddles and were slowly making headway. A boater was nearby and hollered, "you boys having trouble?" We gave him that 'DUH!' look and said, "no sir, just paddling our boat." Our attitudes by this time were turning pretty sour and we were literally burning to a crisp, from head to foot. To keep cool we jumped into the water and propelled the boat by kicking. We did this off and on for a long time, seeming like eternity. We were way overdue at Hall's Boat Dock and Stan alerted Guy about the situation. In a few minutes Guy and his Chris Craft rounded the point. We tied on and he pulled us back to the dock. C. B. and I by now were totally miserable, literally cooked from head to foot.

Growing Pains And Gains

Every inch of our bodies was exposed except that skin protected by our bathing trunks – thank goodness we had sense enough to not take them off when we jumped overboard to cool off. We were miserable many days afterwards. Needless to say, when you are short of wisdom, misery usually follows.

****

Chapter Five

Summers at Rabun Gap

Chapter five

EACH JULY OR AUGUST was summer vacation time and we would go to Granny's place at Rabun Gap, Georgia. Going to the mountains was always an exciting time for family and friends. All looked forward to going with great anticipation. Billy packed his brown leather suitcase several days before we were to go and kept it under his bed. The drive to Rabun Gap was about seventy five miles by automobile and took nearly three hours. U. S. Highway 441, or the Uncle Remus Highway as it was called in the early days, was a very narrow road made of tar and gravel and had its share of potholes.

It was a funny thing about far away places, when you are little everything seemed like a fairyland, far, far away. For instance, Chattanooga, where in the world was that? We always heard about the "Chattanooga Choo Choo," even sang it. Little Rock, Arkansas, gosh that's way away from here. All we knew about Little Rock was they played baseball there. Yellowstone, Grand Canyon, Alaska and Canada were places only to read and dream about. The giant redwoods and sequoias of California made beautiful pictures in the mind but were way too far away for us to ever see them. We were told that if you dig a hole through the center of the earth you would come out in China, Wow! My how times have changed, the world seems to be getting smaller every day. Now with a little patience and resources one can go most anywhere in just a matter of hours.

Located on the Kelly's Creek Road near the Rabun Gap - Nacoochee School was a little mountain, some might call it a little hill but on top of that little mountain sat Granny's summer home. Granddaddy bought the farm in 1915, built the house a year later and named it "Rabun Croft." There were two hundred and twenty five acres that stretched from the Little Tennessee River, crossing the valley and up the side of a large mountain. A large field, presently occupied by the Fruit of the Loom Mill, lay at the foot of the hill and was said to be so fertile it would yield over a hundred bushels of corn per acre without fertilizer. No one ever doubted that - we all considered it a fact. Half of the crop was cut for silage and the rest was left to grow to maturity for feed. As I remember corn was the only crop grown in that field except for the winter cover crops of wheat or rye. Granny's vegetable garden lay between the field and the foot of the little mountain. Just across the York House Road lay the pasture and a large barn with twin silos. There was also a shed for equipment and machinery and a large crib for the corn. Farther up on the side of the mountain was a lush apple orchard and a large spring. The water from the spring would flow for almost the total length of the farm, from high on the mountain to the little mountain supplying all the water needed for the house and farm. That water was so cold it would nearly frost your glass and as Dad said, "would put lead in your pencil." I later learned what that meant, as Brother John, fourteen years younger than me, was born after a summer's vacation. Dad said, "it was that darn mountain water."

The Rabun Gap-Nacoochee School lies to the west of Highway 411 and most eyes that see it are awed by its picturesque beauty. The beautiful school, framed by the surrounding mountains, overlooks the valley and the meandering Little Tennessee River as it flows north through the valley. During the late evening hours the school chimes ring out and resonate throughout the mountains bringing a calming and almost sacred feeling to those who listen.

Another memory was seeing and hearing the Tallulah Falls Railroad steam engine (we called it the Total Failure) as it puffed along the valley floor belching its black smoke in huge puffs and leaving a ribbon of black in its wake. Blowing its whistle, weak at first and growing stronger as it approached each road crossing and before each stop, gave the signal that the mail had arrived at the Rabun Gap Post Office. All that remains of the railroad are spotty traces of the old railroad bed and the giant pillars that supported the long trestle across Tallulah or Nacoochee Lake and the memories of the old trestle near Tiger and the one as it entered Clayton.

∝

During the late 1930s we all rode in the car together and having no air conditioning you can well imagine how uncomfortable that was. But not really, we sang songs and Mother would tell stories and Dad would crack a joke or two and that shortened the trip somewhat. What is an air conditioner anyway? As we neared the small community of Hollywood, Georgia, Dad would say, "Okay boys, look out for Betty Grable, we are going through Hollywood." We all knew the movie star because of her million dollar legs and later as a World War Two pin-up girl.

In 1937 and 1938 the Department of Transportation began construction of a new bridge over the Tallulah River and completed it in 1939. Prior to that time the Tallulah Lake Dam was the highway. The highway narrowed to one lane and each vehicle had to take its turn crossing over the dam. From the dam looking up and seeing the bridge being constructed was enough to convince us boys to say we would never crossover on that thing, if it was ever finished. Well, it was and we did.

In the middle 1940s after we had grown in stature but very little in wisdom, Billy, C. B., Thomas and I would go by bus ahead of Mother and Dad. The only reason I can imagine them letting us do that was perhaps we had outgrown the capacity of the car or maybe we had earned their trust somehow. How we did that I am not sure but had they known we had our twenty two rifles with us, that trust would have quickly shattered. We dismantled our rifles and packed them in our suitcases along with enough ammunition to last our stay. The trip took about a half of a day as it stopped at all the towns and a couple of crossroads. Clayton was a long stopover for passengers to rest and refresh. The bus stop was what is now the Clayton Restaurant located on the main street. We usually got a Pepsi or RC Cola and a bag of salted peanuts and yes, we poured them in our drinks. How else do you eat them? Clayton is six miles south of Rabun Gap but it took about fifteen minutes to get there because of a short stop at Mountain City. By this time we were really anxious to arrive at our destination, the Rabun Gap Post Office at the juncture of Kelly's Creek Road. We walked the final mile or so to the house on the little mountain.

We took the bus on several occasions and I remember one in particular. When we arrived at the house many buzzards were circling high above. We assembled our rifles and climbed out the upstairs bedroom window onto the roof and started firing away at the lazily circling birds. There would be no buzzard on the plate tonight because we never hit one. Thank goodness for that. What the devil would we do with a dead buzzard anyway? Now why was that fun? Heck, I don't know. Maybe we felt like being alone up there put us in charge and besides it was just different.

Mr. C. H. Blalock was the farm manager and called Granny, Ms. Hattie. He always had everything in perfect order when Ms. Hattie came up. Mr. and Mrs. Blalock had a large family and managed the farm as if it belonged to them, which was in accord with the agreement between him and Granddaddy. Mr. Blalock was a man of high integrity and was loved by all. I remember sitting on their porch and eating grapes from the vines growing along the porch trellis and eating fresh Grimes Golden apples straight from the tree. Mrs. Blalock would always greet us with, "children, have chairs." Mother loved sitting in the big rocking chairs and talking to the Blalocks.

Mr. Blalock and Granddad started a herd of Black Angus cows along with several sheep and hogs. Nothing was more peaceful than hearing the far off sound of cowbells ringing and the bleating of the sheep in the cool early hours of the morning. There was a slaughter room in the barn and the Blalocks would process their own meat to sell and for home use and always had fresh ham, beef and lamb when we arrived. Jabal, a colored gentleman, was our favorite farm hand and would supply fresh vegetables from Ms Hattie's garden – tomatoes, beans, squash, potatoes, okra, rhubarb, field corn, grapes and apples. Especially rhubarb, Granny's favorite and she expected it to be the favorite of everyone who sat at her table. It sure wasn't mine. Extending beyond the garden were several apple trees and a couple of grape arbors. To us boys this was surely "The Garden of Eden."

Granny would go to Rabun Croft early and usually requested or rather insisted that Frances and Cousin Tom come up with her. When Billy was a little older he had the honor of going up with them. Billy and Frances insist that there was no honor to it as they dreaded every minute and could not wait until Mother and Dad got there, even though the fact they were there did not change the situation one iota. Granny was still in absolute control. In the corner of the large living room stood a 'hat tree' and several sticks. That was a special corner and each hat and stick fit a certain person's head and hand. Granny would announce – "get your sticks and hats, we are going for a walk." I hated that and do not like organized activities to this day. The adults led the way and we were like little ducklings following along but there was always time for a little mischief.

We had all walked up to the apple orchard, way past the tenant house where the Partains lived. On our return Billy and I were hitting the fence post with our sticks, much to the annoyance of Granny. I was last in line and Billy whacked a post and yellow jackets swarmed, stinging him many times. I think he was the only one that got stung and boy he was covered. Dad carried him to the Partain's house. Mrs. Partain made a soda paste, she called it so'dy and literally covered him with that paste. He looked like something in a horror movie but it did the trick after some minutes of agonizing pain. After that incidence we were very careful as to what we whacked. We learned that it is dangerous out there.

Walking over to the Darnell Creek was always a treat for us boys. It was about a two mile hike over there and back if we went the total distance. Darnell Creek crossed the Kelly's Creek Road about a half of a mile from our gate. As the road to the Darnell

Creek left the main road there was a large yellow buckeye tree and we would all collect a few buckeyes, being careful that they never touched the ground. To pick up a fallen buckeye was bad luck. Always pick them from the tree or bad luck would surely befall you. Then you crossed the ford or the foot log to the other side and the road became a trail that went up following the creek to a beautiful twenty foot waterfall. Native trout abounded in Darnell Creek in the early 1940s and was certainly a pristine part of God's creation. There were many wonderful memories created there. Granny's health was waning and her last years were very sad. Miss Graham, her nurse accompanied her in those years and I believe1938 was Granny's last visit to Rabun Croft. She dearly loved the mountains and nature and I feel that the seed that grew within me came from her and as time went on cultivated my love of nature. Granny's friend, Mrs. Troutman was there that summer as was our family and we all got sick from food poisoning. There was no refrigerator in the mountains in the very early years and foods such as butter, milk and eggs were stored in a drywell. The well was about three feet in diameter and twenty feet deep. It was large enough to handle a screened storage cage. All other items such as meat and cooked leftovers were kept in the ice cabinet on the back porch. The cabinet was cooled by block ice and did a fair job of keeping everything fresh. I recall Dad stopping at a small ice plant as we passed through Clarkesville on our way up. He always left a place for the ice when he packed the car.

On that fateful night I remember we had cured ham and potato salad for supper. Mother and Nurse Graham did not eat any of the ham and it turned out to be the culprit. I always thought the potato salad made us sick and would not eat it for many years. Mother could not convince me to the contrary but it was the ham and now we know that our good Lord was surely looking after us all. Mother and Nurse Graham were truly our guardian angels that night and during the following days. There was no phone service so Dad had to drive over to Dillard to get Doctor Neville. When Dad returned, he was so sick Mother had to help him into the house. Doctor Neville prescribed Milk of

Magnesia and we literally drank that stuff, "til it was running out of our ears." As hard as it was to swallow, it finally did the job. Granny never returned after that year and she passed away in October 1941.

Dad took charge after that and we enjoyed several years of good times. Frances entered high school in 1939 and would invite her girl friends to come up to Rabun Gap. Betty Aderholt, Gene Smith, Mary Alice Griffith, Martha Ann Kelly all loved the place. Mother, as I have said on many occasions, was an angel and could tolerate more than any human I have ever known. She simply could not see the bad in a situation because of all the good she saw. In addition to all those girls, she let Billy and me invite our friends. C. B. was one of her own so she did not consider him a guest. Wherever he went I went and vice versa and usually Thomas would come. Mother loved all of our friends and enjoyed having them with us.

Harry and C. B. paying their way

Frances and her crowd were several years older than we were and as I recall were totally consumed thinking about boys and Frank Sinatra. This was the Sinatra era and all that squealing when they heard him on the radio or played his recordings was totally obnoxious to us. I guess we were totally obnoxious to the girls, being the pests that we were. They would swim and bath in the Little Tennessee River but never without several little eyes peeking at them. You never heard such screaming and squealing when they saw us watching them. I remember one such occasion when the girls were in the river and we sneaked in to the bank and climbed the trees to get a better look. As we did we discovered something much better than girls, there were grapes everywhere and as we were gouging ourselves we kind of became unaware of the girls. They saw us and started their squealing and ranting, threatening us with all kinds of threats, but to no avail, we just kept picking and eating until we could eat no more. Eating grapes was a lot more exciting than a bunch of silly girls splashing around in the river. We made sacks out of our shirts and filled them with grapes and carried them to the house. Lorene Wilhite was our cook at the time and she made fresh grape jelly from our pickings. They were the best tasting grapes you ever put in your mouth, small wild concord grapes growing everywhere on the banks of the Little Tennessee River. It is sad now to see that the bank where we played has been stripped clean of all its trees. Now only weeds grow there.

Lorene Wilhite and her youngest daughter Jackie would come up with us to the mountains each summer. Lorene was our cook and housekeeper and her husband Hoyt was custodian of Martin Institute for many years. Our family loved the Wilhites and when Lorene was no longer able to work her daughter, Hilda, helped Mother with housework and cooking chores.

I recall being in the first grade and one day ran away from school. Hoyt was sitting on the curb eating his lunch and asked me where was I going. I told him I was going home, that I did not like school. He gave me a baloney and biscuit sandwich and as we sat eating our lunch, he convinced me it was best that I go back to school because he surely did not want me to get into trouble. Hoyt was one of those role models that I mentioned earlier.

$$\infty$$

Swimming in the mountains was a lot of fun. We swam most of the time in the Little Tennessee River. The headwaters of the river formed at an elevation of 2,200 feet at the confluence of Keener and Billy Creeks in the Wolf Fork Cove, about five miles from our little mountain. 14/ The River is on the north side of the Blue Ridge Divide and flows from south to north and having a very large watershed was fairly deep as it flows past our little mountain. Most of the time we swam at the bridge where there was a big rock and a good deep hole and the water was so pure the bottom was always visible. Man was it cold! Just a short distance down stream was the confluence of Betty Creek causing the Little Tennessee River to almost double its width. Betty Creek was a good place to play and was an exceptional trout and red eye stream.

$$\infty$$

For Jayne and me, Betty Creek will always be special. It was the summer of 1952 and Jayne was my guest at Rabun Gap. We went for a walk and ended up on the bank of the creek at the junction of the river. How that happened I do not know as it was a rather weedy walk and Jayne did not have a real fondness for snakes. But love is powerful and through the weeds she went. I asked her to marry me on that summer afternoon. She said yes and we married in December of 1953. A beautiful girl on a beautiful day in the beautiful mountains at the juncture of two beautiful streams and a big "YES." Could anything have been better? I think not.

Another place we swam was the Rabun Gap - Nacoochee School swimming pool. Mr. Blalock said it would probably be okay for us to swim there and his word was good enough, so swim we did. The pool did not appear to be used very much during late July and August as most of the students were gone for the summer. That was much to our liking. We would walk over and spend most of the afternoons there. Occasionally Dad would take us to Clayton to the City Pool. Swimming was important but there was so much other stuff to do in the mountains, it just was not like being at home.

For instance, fishing was always on our minds and how we got our bait was somewhat scary and at times very dangerous, even with supervision. We would take a long cane, tie a wad of paper around its end, set it afire and singe the wasps off of their nest. Knock the nest down and you had your bait, nice juicy grubs. Now, that doesn't seem very dangerous but the wasp's nest was usually under the eve of the house and if the flames were held there too long it could mean big trouble. Just a small spark could have been disastrous and I shudder to think about it now. That's where Dad's supervision came in handy.

Another way to get bait, no supervision required was to find a whiteface hornet's nest, knock it down and there you had several layers of juicy grubs. Sounds good but not so easy. The hornet seems to have a built in radar or sonar system and can fly at ultrasonic speeds and make no mistake about it, they know who is holding the pole or who threw the apple at their home and will protect it with wild fury. We quickly learned those facts when we tried to disengage a nest from the lower branch of an apple tree. We were in the upper end of the Garden of Eden. Hanging peacefully in the gentle mountain breeze was a golly whopper of a nest. We began throwing apples at the nest from a distance that proved to be very inadequate. Those hornets came out of that nest and locked onto us like missiles locking on a jet aircraft. I ran up the hill when one of the missiles struck me between the shoulder blades, knocking me flat on my face. I am pretty sure Billy got hit, in fact I think we all did. We stuck to the singeing method after that. Even though it was dangerous, it sure did not hurt as much as the tail end of a hornet did.

I remember on one occasion as we were leaving the road to go over to Betty Creek an older gentleman was walking along and asked us what kind of fish we were trying to catch. We told him trout. He asked what were we using for bait and we told him wasp larva. He said, "You are standing next to the best trout bait there is," and pointed to a gall on a golden rod stem. He cut the gall open with his knife and inside was an inch long worm, the larva of the golden rod moth. He said, "that worm is the best trout bait you can use." We did not have much luck with the worms but we believed the old man anyway as he talked with much authority.

We fished the Little Tennessee most of the time, usually below the bridge on the Dillard road. C. B. caught a very large bream from the bank. Another good trout stream was Darnell's Creek. We caught Kentucky bass or red-eyes just above where the creek entered the river. Trout were more plentiful in the upper part of the creek near the beautiful waterfalls. In the early fifties I fished a small pond on the side of U.S. 441 highway. The pond was about a half acre in size and was created when the Highway Department blasted for stone to be used in the upgrading of the roadbed. I fished the pond with my fly rod using a yellow popping spider. The bass would tear it up and I would usually take home a nice stringer of fish. That was my private little pond and there was absolutely no evidence of anyone else fishing there. The pond is across from the present Osage Farms, Inc. vegetable and fruit Stand. It is well hidden but still there.

Making cider was one of those special things to do on our vacation. Billy, C. B., Thomas and I would arise early in the morning and walk over to the barn. Bob Blalock, the youngest of the Blalock boys would be at the barn hitching the mule to the sled. We would load the sled with several baskets and head up to the orchard. But prior to this preparation, we had to make sure we had enough containers to hold our product. Granny had accumulated many ale bottles over the years. I do not recall seeing her or anyone drinking out of the green bottles stored in the pantry but they were there, dozens of them. When we used them for the current cider year we always rinsed them out and returned them to their rightful place to be used again next year. We checked a couple of days before to make sure they were still there. They were and Dad hauled them over to the barn for us. We used corncobs for corks. After getting to the orchard we picked apples from the ground and from the tree. Green, red and yellow, all kinds and loaded our sled. There were a few rotten spots but that was no problem because they would all be ground together. There were probably some worms but all they ate was apple and as far as we were concerned they were just part of the apple. Doctor Lord always said that the worm in the peach would not hurt you. After all it was full of peach. Peaches/apples, what's the difference and if Dr. Lord said it, then it had to be okay. After filling the baskets we returned to the barn. We washed the apples in the cattle water trough and after removing the trash we carried the washed apples over to the equipment barn where the cider mill was stored. We poured several buckets of water through the mill thinking we were cleaning it thoroughly. Naturally the water came from the cow trough.

Now we were ready to start making cider. Pouring the apples into the turning grinder and seeing the pulp fill the press bucket was fun to watch. After the bucket was full the screw press slowly pressed the pulp into a steady stream of good smelling juice. We strained the juice through a fairly clean cloth into a milk bucket and then slowly into the green ale bottles, finally capping each one with a good fitting corncob. The dry pulp was fed to the hogs. After bottling the cider we took it back to the house and stored it in the large walk-in pantry and that is where our knowledge of cider making ended. All we had was apple juice but it was not pasteurized, therefore much of our juice turned to pure vinegar and sometimes the corncob blew out. It was always a shock to open a bottle of juice and get a mouthful of vinegar. We drank enough of the good and sometimes not so good juice, occasionally giving us another good case of intestinal upheavals.

Our mountain escapades were many and some were on the lighter side such as walking over to Dillard and getting refreshing sodas at the Dillard Drugstore. It was a mile and a half over there on an unpaved road that passed by the Dillard House and what was then the schoolhouse and is now the City Hall. There were two brick columns there that we loved to climb. How we got to the top of them, I do not know for they stand about four feet square and maybe seven feet tall. Boys will be boys.

There was a time in my early days when I aspired to be an artist. I guess I was being overcome by nature and was inspired to capture on canvas what I saw. That's an artist term for drawing a picture. On one particular morning I walked, with my art supplies in hand to the gate at the bottom of the hill. There was a stone wall about four feet high and twenty feet in length. I climbed onto the wall and from there was a good view of the barn and the beautiful mountains in the background. Rabun Bald is Georgia's second highest peak and was clearly visible in the distance. To the northwest you could see the Rabun Gap-Nacoochee School in the foreground and in the background was Piggins Nose, in North Carolina. We called it, Pickin - His - Nose. Beauty was in every direction. I tried to capture the barn and Rabun Bald in my inspired painting. Everybody bragged on my work, of course, because I was so young, trying to encourage me in my new endeavor. Mother even hung it on the wall for all to see, I guess proving that little white lies can be useful in keeping a little ones interest at its peak. It did not work in my case as art fell by the wayside but my love for nature in all aspects flourished and continues to grow today.

According to Dad, I caught my first trout when I was five years old. Most of us cannot remember many things that took place in those early years of our lives. But I do recall a couple of dramatic happenings at that time in my life and this is one of them. Granny wanted to go on a picnic at one of her favorite places - a place in the north end of Wolf Fork Cove on Rickman's Creek. I remember our whole family driving a good way off of the main road up a rocky lane to a pasture. I remember Ms. Marie Dumas was with us. Marie was a professor of English at the University of Georgia and a dear friend of the family. The pasture had many exposed rocks as if the soil had been blown from them and there were small islands of stunted trees dotting the landscape, surviving only in the thin soil because of the abundant mountain rainfall. We were at an elevation of around 2,300 feet and the head of Rickman Creek was a good distance above us.14/ The creek cascaded down over the exposed shoals as it plummeted, fast and cold to the Little Tennessee River below. Billy and I were playing on the rocks under the watchful eye of the grownups and saw a fish in a small pool on the edge of the creek. It swam under the overhang of the rock, and I ran back to Dad and told him what we had seen. He found a short stick and Granny gave him a safety pin from her inner garment. He made a hook and tied it to a string that one of the ladies had, probably Granny because she was mighty frugal and saved everything. He completed my first fishing pole and went with me to where we had seen the fish. With his help I put the hook in the water and the current took it right under the lip of the rock where the fish had gone. I gave a jerk and hung the fish in its side, a trout. It was a whopper, all five inches of it. Mother cleaned a pickle jar for my trophy and I carried it back to the house and put it in a washtub. It lived a couple of days and died.

All good things have to end and the old gang began to drift apart. Billy graduated from high school in 1947 and C. B. and Thomas in 1948 and this sadly made the two years difference in our ages much more significant. I was like a stick floating freely with the current and suddenly being swept into an eddy and not being a part of the flow anymore. Girls, cars, college and new interest crept out of nowhere and began to pull us in different directions.

But things have a way of working out, as they always do. Sidney Johnson and Dick Copas were already good friends and came to the mountains for several more summers. Sidney was a daredevil and Dick was a comedian and that combination made quite a team. I will never forget Dick's imitation of "Woody Woodpecker." He kept us laughing most of the time. Dad said those boys could eat more white bread than anybody he had ever seen. Jayne and I were dating in 1949 and Bill and Marie and the girls, Wylie and Shirley, Henry and Martha Jean would come up and we had some really good times. Granddaddy and Mudder, Mother's mom and dad, came down from Washington, D. C. and stayed for a couple of summers and that was always a pleasant time in our lives.

Another yellow jacket incident happened when Granddaddy and Brother John were walking outside the house. John was a little thing, could not have been more than five or six years old. He was walking along holding Granddaddy's hand and swinging a cowbell. All of a sudden the air was full of swarming yellow jackets. John was stung many times but it could have been much worse had he not dropped the cowbell. It fell in the upright position completely covering and blocking the hole. Miraculously, Granddaddy did not get the first sting.

Jayne recalls during one summer when we were all up there she gave Mudder a permanent and when she applied the solution to her hair the iron in the water reacted with the chemicals and turned it purple. Thinking Mudder's hair was ruined and not knowing what to do, she proceeded with the permanent and during the final rinsing the purple disappeared. You can imagine the sigh of relief form both Jayne and Mudder and all of us for that matter. It sure would not look right having a purple hair Grandmother running around up there.

In 1955 I was drafted into the Army and was home on leave after finishing basic training. Dad and Jayne drove me to the Atlanta Airport for my departure to El Paso – Fort Bliss, Texas -

Nike Missile School. On the way over Dad told us that he had made the decision to sell Rabun Croft because of management difficulties, and how he hated to have to tell us because he knew how much we loved the place. He explained that he had signed an "option to sell" with the Robert and Company Associates of Atlanta, Georgia and this proposed sale would bring employment to many people in the area and Rabun County. The deal was finalized in 1956. Jayne and I stayed there for our final time in the summer of 1955 just before starting my tour of duty in the Army. Thus ending an era in our lives that we were truly blessed to have been a part of, an era that included family and friends and all that remember "Rabun Croft." All is gone now except for the Little Mountain with its circling narrow road and the two silos standing on the eastside where the barn once stood. But the memories of all the good times will live on as long as there are ears to hear.

****

Chapter Six

❧

The Evolution of Smoking

Chapter six

Tobacco is a dirty weed.
I like it.
It satisfies no normal need.
I like it.
It makes you thin:
It makes you lean:
It takes the hair right off your bean:
It's the worst darn stuff I've ever seen.
I like it. – Anonymous

I SHALL NEVER FORGET how and where it all began. A friend, I will call him Butch for the sake of anonymity, came to visit his grandparents as he had done many times before. We played with him on each of his visits but this one was different, much different. Butch introduced us to the dirty weed tobacco but I hold no animosity toward him. If he had not done this, someone else would have. The temptation to smoke was very close at hand. After all we had tried corn silk and rabbit tobacco. Cigarette smoking in those days was seemingly the natural thing to do.

The radio and television commercials were so enticing, who could resist? Some even suggested that smoking was good for your health. As I recall, the only deterrent heard to keep a young person from smoking was, "cigarettes will stunt your growth." That really was pretty weak because it was said about coffee and tea and we all knew that was not right. Remember little Johnny, the hotel page and his "Call for Phillip Morris ---," or the billboard stating, "I would walk a mile for a Camel," and hearing, "the cool refreshing feel to your throat of Kool Cigarettes" and "L.S.M.F.T." - Lucky Strike Means Fine Tobacco. Radio and later television were saturated with commercials telling how great it was to smoke. Popular entertainers advertised for their favorite cigarette or so they made us believe they were their favorite. Arthur Godfrey made Chesterfield the smoker's smoke and then there was Perry Como's hype for Camels and Bing Crosby always had his pipe that he seemed to really enjoy. Most of the men smoked back then, it was just the manly thing to do and soon the women caught on, which was not a ladylike thing to do. In the movies it was cool to see our soldiers sitting in the foxhole enjoying a smoke between battles and the act of chivalry as the gentleman lit the ladies cigarette. Even the cowboys in the old west enjoyed their smoke at times. Buck Jones always slipped a piece of gum in his mouth before each shoot out with the outlaws and I don't recall seeing Hop-along Cassidy ever smoking. They were the exception.

I remember seeing a cowboy sitting on his horse, kind of sideways in his saddle, with one leg crossed and rolling a cigarette with one hand. Now that was a challenge for any red - blooded boy, even without a horse. He then whipped out a match and struck it on the saddle horn.

There were no ready rolled cigarettes out on the range. Tobacco came in little bags that had a drawstring and a pack of cigarette papers stuck in the label, just like our Bull Durham or Duke's Mixture of today. The cowboy opened the bag with two fingers, poured tobacco and spread it evenly onto a cigarette paper, pulled the drawstring with his teeth to close the bag, rolled the cigarette, licked the seam and twisted the end to keep the tobacco from falling out. He then struck the match by holding it tightly and nicking the head of it with his thumbnail or struck it on his butt. There was an art to doing that, one we could never master. Don't bite your fingernails if you want to be successful at doing that.

C. B., Billy, Thomas, Butch and I were in our hideout and it was a very good hideout. In fact we had several but this one was unique. The Will's and the Lord's garages were side by side with about three feet of space separating them. We bored holes in the side of Doctor Lord's garage so we could see who was coming. That was the traffic side and we needed to know where the intruder was and how long we had to be quiet. Garages did not have windows and usually only little boys, cats, dogs and other varmints went under or between them so we felt really secure. But that security was about to be compromised. It was done the instant Butch pulled out a pack of cigarettes he had hidden in his shirt and lit one. Then passed it around for each of us to try. Now, (dadgoneit,) that is one word, we not only had to be quiet but we had the smell of tobacco to contend with. He inhaled and even blew a smoke ring or two. Butch was a pro, we could see immediately that this boy had been at it for awhile. Each time the cigarette came around Butch tried to coax us to inhale but it was not a matter of teaching, it was more like building a tolerance to do it without passing out. After about a couple of passes the oxygen in our brains had been replaced with carbon monoxide and our heads were spinning like a top. The purity of our bodies had been compromised. We were on the verge of passing out and felt like we might die but it all passed and we were hooked. The stink of tobacco was in the air and on our clothes and breath. To smoke or not to smoke was not a decision, it just happened. We began smoking and now a whole new era had dawned.

We were back at it in no time and steadily sinking deeper and deeper into trouble. Our sisters, Frances and Linda had entered the picture. They would catch us time and time again by simply smelling us but that did not deter us. We were hooked, sneaking around and swiping cigarettes whenever we could. Little did we know at the time though that we were totally hooked. I guess we thought we could quit at anytime but this turned out to be the most terrible time during our growing up years. It really hurts to write these words today because of our stupidity but it was part of growing up. We tried to quit many times. We tried cold turkey and we tried the buddy system, even writing an oath pledging to quit. We rolled the oaths in a neat tight roll and placed them under one of the tar expansion joints between a concrete section on the newly paved Gainesville Highway. We selected an expansion joint down near the driveway to the Clifford Storey house. I suppose they are still there today if the original concrete is still in place.

Yes, we tried to quit many times but were just unable to do so. When we could not find a good cigarette butt to smoke we resorted to other things. Corn silk and rabbit tobacco were old standbys and worked pretty good but we tried other things like dried pear leaves, dead grape or muscadine vines and even coffee. If we ever had a penny or two we could always go down to Mr. Baxter's store and get a couple of cigarettes there but we had to find someone older to buy them for us. Of course we had to pay him to do it for us. Usually one cigarette did the job. It usually worked out pretty well. A funny thing about smoking was the fact that we did not smoke unless there were two of us or we were all together. I guess it was more fun that way or maybe it was a way for us to hone our skills in craftiness, in other words how not to get caught.

After Martin Institute burned and was demolished workers came in to salvage the bricks. For days and weeks they cleaned the brick by chipping the concrete from them. They stacked them in huge stacks to be picked up at a later date. Those stacks provided an almost perfect place to hide our tobacco products. We would pull out a brick or two and stuff our Dukes mixture or Bull Durham or whatever into the space and put a half brick in place to seal the tobacco tomb. Ingenious we thought, except when it rained and ruined everything. Our garage hiding places became inadequate because of the smoke and stink of tobacco. Again the stacks of salvaged bricks came into play. Along the front of the school ruins was a walkway extending to the right and left of the front entrance. Evergreen trees or junipers were planted along the walks and were only partially killed by the fire. The workers had made stacks of brick parallel with the walk and unknowingly had created excellent hiding places for us. The stack was about five feet high and was fairly long. No one ever came close to that area as it was very near the ruins. One day we were there smoking and playing and all of a sudden there was this distinct put-put-put-put-puttering sound and someone said in a loud whisper, "be quiet, a tractor is coming!" We all laughed and assured him that there was no tractor coming, it was just our "champion pooter," doing his thing again. Now that's a guilt feeling if there ever was one. When you are doing wrong, you are always looking over your shoulder.

Underneath the Old Tin Gymnasium was a good hideout but it was just too wide open and anyone who happened to walk by could easily see what was going on underneath. Our neatest hideout was in a culvert underneath the street. Down at the intersection of Church and College Street is a culvert about three feet in diameter and we would sneak into the lower end, crawl in a few feet and smoke away. No one would ever figure that one out. We were perfectly safe and secure. You did not want to be in there when it rained though because it's amazing how much water and trash can come through those things when a toad stringer - gulley washer comes down. Another good hiding place was between the hedge and Mr. Mobley's garage. There was a curb about knee high along the property line. We sat on the curb and smoked until one day Mrs. Elrod saw our smoke from her kitchen window and hollered at us. That was the end of that hiding place-foiled again by the smoke.

Smoking caused all kind of problems. Being afraid of getting caught was the number one worry and it also required money to finance our habit. Our needs were met for awhile anyway because of an accumulated treasure waiting to be found. When the old gymnasium was built in the 1920s funds were in short supply, causing it to be somewhat crude with lots of cracks. The bleachers were located on the north, south and east sides and had many cracks in them. Those cracks created the treasure that was there to be found. Many pennies, nickels, dimes, some quarters and an occasional fifty cent piece escaped from their owners pockets and fell through the cracks. We only had to take our flashlights and scavenge under the bleachers and count our newly discovered windfall. I am not sure who came up with that one but it sure paid off.

Cigarettes came in all sizes to satisfy every taste. There was Chesterfield, Camels, Lucky Strikes and regular Kools for those who wanted a short smoke. Then there was the Herbert Taryeton, king size Kools, Pall Malls and Wings for those who liked the long cigarette. I think Wings were our favorite because the wing on the package looked prestigious, like maybe pilots smoked them or maybe they were cheaper. Probably the latter was the reason for our choice. We steered clear of the Picayune and Home Run. Those things were cheap but powerful and certainly not for boys to mess around with, kind of like comparing dynamite to a firecracker.

Roll your own cigarettes came in cloth bags or tinfoil bags. Dukes Mixture and Bull Durham were probably the most popular and there was Kite tobacco, laced with menthol to give it a cool and soothing taste. Pipe tobacco fell into the specialty class. It came in tins, bags, kegs or humidors and in sheets. The sheet tobacco was to be crumbled and placed into the pipe at the leisure of the smoker. Edgeworth and Hale were popular sheet tobaccos and were pretty strong. I remember when C. B. and I swiped some sheet tobacco from Dad's dresser. It was in a small tin box and was a very dark, almost black tobacco. We were sitting on the running board of Granny's 1939 Dodge, the "Chariot" as Dad called it. The Chariot was parked in our backyard after Granny passed away. We crumbled some of the tobacco into one of Dad's pipes and lit it. After we each took a drag or two it hit us like a sledgehammer right between the eyes. It made us mighty sick for a short while but plenty long enough to cure us from ever sucking that egg again. It was some kind of Turkish tobacco that would put the Home Run cigarette to shame.

Then there were those ever tempting, good smelling cigars. Kipling once said, "And a woman is only a woman but a good cigar's a smoke." The popular brands were Hav-a-Tampa, Tampa Nuggets and the cheap rum soaked Crook cigar. Occasionally we tried one or two of the Crook. I think it was called crooks because of the worm like curves of its shape. The Crook came in packs of five and was cheap but very mild for a cigar.

One can not talk about tobacco without mentioning snuff and chewing tobacco. Snuff was not used much in our circle and about the only snuff product I remember was Rooster. We made our own snuff at times by mixing coco with sugar and did a little dipping. I bet every kid in America pretended to dip snuff using coco and sugar. Chewing tobacco was a different thing. It came in twists, bags and plugs. Beechnut looked like pre-chewed tobacco and was popular for those who wanted a wad to tuck between the cheek and gum but the plug and the home twist was the real man's chewing tobacco. "Gimme a cut off of your plug or twist," was common and usually the owner of the plug would oblige. I particularly remember the honey colored Honeydew plug tobacco. A bunch of us were on the square one Saturday night and there was an older gentleman there. He had just cut a chunk off his plug and slipped it into his mouth. He saw me watching and offered me a small piece. I took it trying to be sociable and let it wallow around in my mouth for a few seconds and soon had the urge to spit. The old man said, "swallow, it won't hurt you." That was bad advice, I did as he said and swallowed it, tobacco and all. I turned green as the algae in a stagnant pond and sick as a dog. My only try at chewing tobacco was then and there. Maybe it was good advice because I never tried chewing again.

Speaking only for myself I had many regretful years to follow, trying to quit the filthy habit on many occasions but not able to overcome its addiction. In my later years I decided to attend a quit smoking seminar. This was one of those hypnosis seminars and was only successful in that it caused a simple but dramatic change in my attitude. It put me in charge of my life by not letting a filthy little weed control my actions. I beat the habit twenty two years ago and as I look back I can only ask, "why did we ever smoke in the first place?" There is no doubting it. Smoking was the dumbest things we ever did. It was a job in itself and a very expensive habit. Only after quitting did I realize how obnoxious I was to my family, friends and to so many others and also how harmful it was to our bodies. We were getting along pretty good until that day between the garages and now, oh how we wish it never happened but it did and became one of our growing pains and upon quitting, a definite gain.

******

Chapter Seven

The War Days

Chapter seven

PATRIOTISM AS DEFINED IN Webster's dictionary is "devoted love, support, and defense of one's country: national loyalty." Make no doubt about it, World War Two with Germany, Italy and Japan awakened and gave many persons, young and old, in this great nation of ours a passion to be a part of that conflict, whether great or small. A passion to crush our enemies at all cost, but as one would expect there was a fair amount of opposition against going to war, as is usually the case with all wars. The European war with Germany and Italy officially began in 1939 but due to opposition the United States did not enter it officially until after the December 7, 1941 sneak attack on Pearl Harbor by the Japanese. However, prior to that time we were supporting Great Britain by shipping supplies for their war efforts against Nazi Germany. Germany strategically blocked all shipping lanes to Great Britain with their submarines trying to strangle her into surrender. German submarines torpedoed a couple of our navy escort ships killing many sailors but America still remained neutral. President Roosevelt had repeatedly said America would not fight on foreign soil. However, the attack on Pearl Harbor changed that and a few days after the attack, Germany and Italy declared war against the United States. Now we were fighting on two fronts and continued to ship war supplies to England

and Russia. My Uncle Joe Woodward, Mother's brother, was a seaman aboard the merchant ship USS Quadulene and was in harms way many times crossing waters infested with enemy submarines. Uncle Joe was my true personal hero as were the many local young men who served during the war. Particularly those closest to us were Morris Bryan, Jr., Stuart Lord, Damon Gauze, Thomas Benton, Bobby Bailey, Bill Knight, Gene Yearwood, Hillyer Johnson, Vernon Carter and Britt Elrod.

At the Saturday movies we were really exposed to the war in grim detail. The short newsreel at the beginning of the movie kept us well informed. I shall never forget seeing how the Japanese soldiers treated the women and children, especially the babies when they overran the villages of the Pacific Islands. Those images of the atrocities, cruelty, viciousness and hate of the war were permanently etched into my memory and I feel sure that those newsreels fueled the patriotism of many and helped in part to bring the war to its end.

�֍

We had already begun to see quite a few changes taking place in our lives, those of sacrifice and of doing without many common goods that we were accustomed to having. War posters were everywhere urging everyone to conserve many things because they were essential to the war effort. We can all remember the "Uncle Sam Wants You" poster. Uncle Sam, with that red white and blue top hat, sternly looking and pointing a finger in your face certainly got the attention of those for whom it was intended. "Rosie the Riviter," that sexy lady standing there with the big rivet gun in her hand let everyone know that the factories and the war machines were in full swing. As a Japanese officer said of the sneak attack on Pearl Harbor, "we have awakened a sleeping giant," or something to that affect. He was dead on the head with that statement. The giant never yawned as it arose and immediately went to work destroying its enemy.

Later as the war raged on rationing began in a big time way. It seems most things in those days were red, white and blue, mostly red and blue. There were red and blue tokens, red and blue coupons and certificates for all sorts of things such as gasoline, nylon, tires, cigarettes and foods of all sorts - sugar, butter, canned goods, beef, chocolate and coffee. America adjusted and quickly came up with substitutes for food items. For instance, honey took the place of sugar, Postum and Ovaltene replaced coffee and margarine replaced butter, and do you remember the "Tasty Yeast" candy bar? As I recall they were about a half of an inch thick and three quarters of an inch wide and maybe three and a half inches long. It seemed to satisfy our taste for chocolate and we still had the old favorites, B-B bat and the Sugar Daddy.

Margarine came in a special squeeze bag with a little package of coloring. It was fun to pour in the coloring and start squeezing until it was a creamy yellow and you knew it was mixed thoroughly. It was then put in a mold and into the refrigerator to become firm and ready for use. Billy and I usually volunteered to do the mixing and at times things got a little out of control when it turned into a football game. Man, it would have been a total mess if that bag had broken.

Mayonnaise was made using a quart size jar churn. The jar stood about ten inches and had a screw on cap with a plunger. Mother prepared the mix and put it in the jar, then screwed on the funnel like cap and plunger and Billy or I slowly poured in the oil while she churned. We soon had a good rich homemade mayonnaise.

Cigarettes were available but sometimes hard to get as most went to our troops. Remember when Lucky Strike's green went to war because the pigment in the ink was vital to the war effort? Tinfoil was used to line the cigarette package, chewing gum wrappers, candy wrappers and many food items and was discontinued because it, too, was vital. How many kids do you reckon made their baseballs with a ball of tinfoil wrapped with friction tape? You could literally knock the cover off of that one. Gasoline was rationed to just a few gallons each week for going to church, to see the doctor and any emergency that might arise. Tires were made from real rubber and were also rationed. Soon, synthetic rubber was discovered and turned out to be superior to the real thing. The list went on and on.

Everyone was encouraged to buy U. S. Saving Bonds to help finance the war effort. Messages over the radio were constantly pounding the people, kids alike to buy them and many did because all were affected and wanted to be a part of the war effort. Hollywood entertainers held benefits and posters were everywhere urging us to buy war bonds. Investing in America was a very successful program, helping to raise millions of dollars.

There was much talk about "Victory Gardens" and Billy and I thought, surely we could do that. All it took to accomplish that task was a spot in the backyard, a few seed, a shovel, a small amount of guana fertilizer, remember that stinky stuff, and a mattock. Dad selected our spot next to the garage. It received a fair amount of sun in the morning hours but was shaded in the afternoon by the large chinaberry tree, privet shrubs and the garage. It appeared to be an okay spot and we loved the shade, so we began to prepare the ground. We already knew from our backyard swimming pool experience that digging was not so easy as we could barely lift the mattock and did not weigh enough to push the shovel into the ground. John McColloch, our yardman, gave us a little of his time and helped to get us started. We were able to prepare enough ground to plant some radishes, carrots and turnips and a couple of cabbage plants. To make a long story short, I think all we harvested was a few very hot radishes and rabbits ate the cabbage. Our good intentions did not help the war effort, but we tried.

I remember going to the "canning plant," located at the intersection of Hill and Elm Street and helping Mr. McMullen carry supplies and do odd jobs for the ladies as they canned their fruits of harvest. The "Victory Gardens," were a huge success and the canning plant was able to operate without restrictions during the war. Jayne and Shirley recall spending many hot July and August days helping their mothers, preparing vegetables and doing odd jobs.

The ladies of the town did a lot of knitting during the war. I recall Billy and I holding our arms up with hands pointed out, thumbs up and fingers closed together and Mother taking her yarn in wide loops and placing it across our hands. She would then begin to wrap the yarn into cantaloupe size balls for easy handling. She would ball up different colors and knit squares to be sent somewhere to be made into wool articles for the overseas troops. I think that was a Red Cross project. There must have been millions of those squares made and sent abroad. The ladies would also organize groups to make "care packages" for the troops.

Down at the old depot and between Kinney's seed treatment facility and the old canning plant was where scrap iron was purchased for the war effort. I do not recall the gentleman's name and can't remember how much he paid per pound but I do remember that he had a gigantic pile of scrap and for a short while scrap iron became our business.

We scoured our backyards and the entire neighborhood filling our wagons with whatever we could find. Eventually the whole town was canvassed. We even pulled our wagons along the railroad track picking up loose spikes, connector plates and even tried to pick up a short piece of rail or two, always being very careful not to cause a train derailment. We also went to the dirtiest spots in town – behind Jefferson Motor Company's Service garage and Kelly's garage. Both places had heaps of greasy scrap metal that had been thrown behind the buildings. Now that was a mess and it did not take us long to realize that bonanza, even though it was a gold mine, was not worth the outcry that would meet us at home. We figured we might be banned from our families had we shown up looking like grease monkeys. Another source for scrap was old abandoned street signposts. If the post just stood there not saying anything, would anyone care if it disappeared? Even property corners came under our scrutiny.

Every little thing helped and I shall never forget when Mr. McMullen appointed Billy, Thomas and C. B. to be airplane spotters. I think Mr. Mac was our official Civil Defense Director or official Air Raid Warden. I was too young to be a spotter but never the less was proud to tag along. They were given a little slide rule like thing with pictures of the enemy planes on them and there were several holes of all sizes on it. We would sit in the old school ruins for hours spotting planes. When you spotted one, you would look through the hole that the image filled and somehow calculate its distance and elevation. If it was an enemy plane you reported it to Mr. Mac. By then the plane was clean out of sight but no matter, no one ever saw an enemy plane but it sure made three and one half boys feel big and proud.

All through the war years and especially 1942 and 1943 there were army convoys constantly passing through Jefferson. There were jeeps, supply trucks, personnel trucks and all kinds of equipment moving north to south along U. S. Highway 129. We would all gather on the Lyle's lawn and yell and wave to the GIs as they passed. But the girls, being as silly as a bunch of geese and the fact that they were juniors and seniors in high school, threw kisses and screamed like we had never heard before. Golly, that was embarrassing. It was almost like they were in the presence of old blue eyes, Frank Sinatra. The GIs threw notes with their addresses on them, rolled up and stuffed into empty rifle shell cases. Each time one was thrown the screaming would start and when one was caught you would think it was a precious stone or something. Crazy!

When we went to Athens during those years checking on Granny's house, Mother and Dad would take us over to Sunset and Oglethorpe. There was a large field at the intersection that was used by the troops as a bivouac area. It was very impressive to see the pup tents lined up in precision row after row and the sentries walking their post. It made us feel proud and safe.

We sang a lot during the war days, especially while traveling in the car. Songs like, Over there, over there, we're coming over; We did it before and we can do it again; Praise the Lord and pass the ammunition; "Don't sit under the apple tree with anyone else but me; Coming in on a wing and a prayer; Bugle Boy of company B, and G. I. Jive - man alive, just to name a few. It was the time of two of my favorites, Johnny Mercer and Hoagy Carmichael and it was the big band era. Glen Miller was a favorite of everyone and unfortunately died while in the service entertaining the troops. He was a true hero and there will never be another like him. Those were good entertainers, singing and playing good songs to make things better for our GIs and all of us at home.

As I look back music was a good part of our lives. The old victrola or phonograph at Rabun Croft played those hard rubber 78 r.p.m records. With a few turns of the crank on the side of the victrola we would sit back and listen to tunes such as: My prayer; A tisket, a tasket, a brown and yellow basket; and Hey boys, get away from the wagon wheel, you'll get smut on your clothes. Now those were real 1920s thrillers for sure.

We spent many hours at C. B's house playing records and everybody's favorite was "The Holy City," and I remember "Tweedle O twill, plucking a daisy." It's funny how you remember those things. At home we played a variety of records. The big band music of Benny Goodman, Glen Miller, Sammy Kaye, Tommy Dorsey and Harry James were favorites of all. Dad had his special record, "The Donkey Serenade," and a couple of my favorites were Nelson Eddy and Jeanette McDonald's "Dessert Song and Indian Love Call." Mother liked them all but her special music was that of the 1920s and 30s. Frances had to have all of the Frank Sinatra recordings she could get and those of any other crooner of the time. Togetherness like that was the cement that bonded families and friends together. We can all remember Frances' rendition of "It takes a knock knee'd woman and a bowlegged man, to do the boogie woogie in a frying pan." Now that was a performance. We would like to see her do it now but she might break a hip.

As the war progressed, several war movies were made and shown at the Roosevelt Theater. Sargent York, starring Gary Cooper depicting his heroic escapades during World War One,

Bataan, starring Robert Taylor, Wake Island and Guadacanal were some of our favorites. After we saw a movie we made believe that we were fighting with our troops.

Our battleground was in an isolated part of the school woods, located between Treasure Island and where the Bobby Baileys now live. A place we called the "gulley." The gulley was an eroded part of the old field where pine trees were planted at the turn of the decade and far removed from people. It was a place where we had total freedom and could make as much noise as was necessary to defeat the Germans and Japanese. To be able to do that was very important. Guns make a lot of noise, especially machine guns, hand grenades and exploding bombs and artillery. Usually our rifles were sticks and our handguns were a good cap gun. If we lost our handgun the finger made a fine substitute. Hand grenades could be anything the size of a baseball, such as dirt clods, rocks, etc. but the best and the ones that did the most damage were magnolia cones. A soldier could carry a lot of those with him. It was very important to know the sounds of the different weaponry. For instance, incoming artillery shells and bombs were a high pitch whistle and a good scratchy boom made deep down in the throat. Machine guns were at-at-at-at-at-at-at made in the throat or a continuous trrrrrrrrrrrrrrrrrrr made by slightly lifting the tongue and blowing through slightly open lips. Rifles and handguns were a simple pow, pow or tow, tow. The pow, pow was made with the lip movement and tow, tow was made with a tongue movement. In order to survive it was imperative that you know these things.

Coach Hardin came to our school beginning the 1943/44 class and apparently was a veteran. He and some of his students constructed an obstacle course or a confidence course down and through the school woods. Two of its greatest challenges were the foot log across the ravine. The log was a good twenty five feet across and about fifteen feet to the bottom. The other was an inverted 'v' frame with cross bars from top to bottom on each side.15/ Both of those obstacles were very scary, especially to us boys. We ran the course many times and in fact, we used the foot log later as a part of our normal trail. Why go down and under when you could confidently cross a foot log? Thanks Coach!

To make up for the labor shortage during the war days the schools would let the students go to those farms that needed help to harvest their cotton. The farmers would call the school requesting the help and the school would bus us to the farm. I think I can truly say that I had rather be in school because picking cotton is not an easy way to increase the change in a little one's pocket. I recall going out to Mr. Charlie Sailors and bringing home a total of thirty six cents. That was probably about sixteen pounds worth of cotton. I am sure Mr. Charlie was glad to see some of us leave his place. I do not recall being invited back to help out.

Jayne tells of going out with Shirley to pick cotton for Mr. Y. D. Maddox. The heat was too much for Jayne so she spent most of the afternoon under the shade tree. She had picked a grand total of ten cents worth. That night at supper her Dad said, "well young lady, you did not make enough to even pay for your lunch." I do not think she was called back either.

I do not recall much about the war in Europe ending or "VE Day" but I do recall the end of the Pacific war with Japan. I remember hearing of Colonel Doolittle's B-25 bomber - incendiary raid on Tokyo in an attempt to bring Japan to surrender. We were at Rabun Croft on August 6, 1945, when we heard over the radio, that an atomic bomb was successfully dropped on Hiroshima. Three days later a second bomb was dropped on Nagasaki. The Japanese finally surrendered on September 2, 1945.

Billy and Frances were returning home on the train after visiting Granddaddy and Mudder in Washington, D. C. Frances recalls that it was total chaos on the train after the announcement of victory in Japan or "VJ Day." Soldiers were drunk, people were dancing in the aisles and all kind of crazy things going on. She said it was wild and scary at times because everyone was completely out of control but they made it home okay.

The "Atomic Age" was beginning and as time passed the more destructive weapon was discovered: the " hydrogen bomb." It was not long until Russia, playing catch up made nuclear bombs. We were now clearly in the "nuclear age," and that is when the world really got scary. Talk of backyard bomb shelters was common place, air raid drills were held in our schools and sometime in the early fifties the First Baptist Church was designated as Jefferson's official "air raid shelter" and as far as I know, holds that distinction to this day.

Sometime just before the war ended or soon after a U. S. Army transport plane crashed into the side of Rabun Bald. I was almost thirteen years old but was deemed too young to go up there that morning. Dad, Billy, Mr. Blalock and a couple of his boys went and upon their return as they described the crash I was certainly glad I did not go. During our early Martin Institute and war days the government had accumulated a surplus of food and found it necessary to distribute it to the schools. They distributed all kinds of food: canned beans, dry beans, canned meats, grapefruit, prunes, raisins, bananas, oranges, white rice, brown rice and cheese. I think it was called commodity food.

I could understand why they gave away brown rice because nobody in their right mind would eat that stuff. I can tolerate it now but I still prefer white rice. Jayne recalls eating pinto beans and cornbread in the old tin gymnasium but I never did that. I went home for lunch. After all our house was just across the street from the school and I had rather have a peanut butter and jelly sandwich any day.

The war days were terrible for all and caused much loss and suffering for many families. Our total losses were heavy and horrible and the greatest lesson learned by young and old, I would hope is - "Freedom is not free and should never – never be taken for granted and the memory of our fallen comrades will forever be remembered."

****

Chapter Eight

∝

Guns-Frog Gigging-Hunting and Fishing

Chapter eight

DURING THE LATE 1940s and into the 1950s our attention turned to hunting, fishing and frog gigging. This was a time as different as day and night compared to the way things are today. In 1950 the U. S. population was one hundred and fifty million people and now that figure is over three hundred million. 16/ Farming was the way of life and land values were very low. Farms ranged from a few acres to several hundred, therefore the rural population was very dispersed creating many hunting opportunities. The acres that were not in cropland were either pasture or woodlands. Most farmers did not mind hunters coming on their lands and would cordially say, "just be mindful of the cows." Hardly anyone posted their properties back then and there was no such thing as a sub-division.

Farming was in full force and much corn, grain and cotton was grown along with hogs, cows and chickens. The chickens ran free in the barnyards and cotton was "King of the Crops" but the chicken industry was beginning to take hold and many farmers were switching over to contract growing. Chickens would soon become the leading cash crop and the new King.

The air was fresh and the water was pure and every farm had an old dug well, maybe fifteen to thirty feet deep and thirty or so inches across, usually in the backyard or on the back porch. The well cover was pushed back and the old wooden bucket would be lowered down into the water, given a little slack and lifted by hand making sure the bucket was full. Then a bucket of fresh, cool, sparkling water was cranked up and ready for drinking, either from the old gourd or a well used dented aluminum dipper but only after swishing a little water around to rinse it out. I guess figuring a little bit of somebody else's spit never hurt anyone.

It is a rare thing to find an old usable well like that these days as most are drilled and are much deeper plus the fact that much of our ground water is not so pure anymore. I recall when we were in the Boy Scouts we were told that a free running creek or branch purified itself every twelve feet or so of its flow. That is definitely not true today and was not back then if the stream ran through a pasture. I can attest to that as being true from a later experience.

Guns

Guns were popular with the young and old and most every boy owned a twenty two rifle for squirrel and rabbit hunting or just plinking. Gun paranoia did not seem to exist and most of us had no formal training in gun care and safety. We learned a lot about that from the magazine Boy's Life and the popular hunting and fishing magazines, Field and Stream, Outdoor Life and Sports Afield and while in the Boy Scouts. Most of our training came from our Dads and or an older friend, as was my case with Britt Elrod. Britt taught me how to clean guns, blue a gun barrel, refinish a blemished stock, gun safety, how to use a rifle sling, how to properly cross a fence with a gun and a great deal more. He was a Sargent during World War Two and assigned to training new troops in the proper care and use of weapons. I consider myself lucky to have had his expertise for my learning experiences. Regardless how or from whom we learned, the one liners that stuck in our minds are, "never point a gun at anything you do not intend to shoot, never," and "never assume a gun is unloaded, always check to make sure."

Britt and I would go over to the old track field and target practice or go out to the their farm off the Commerce highway. We went down on the small creek and he would place washers on the bank. The washers had holes in the center somewhat larger than the diameter of a twenty two bullet and that hole was our target. Now you cannot go out and target practice like that anymore because of too many homes, sub-divisions, schools and other populous. It is much too dangerous and I miss not being able to do that today.

The school woods was another popular place for target practice. Firing into an old very large fire-scarred white oak made a good safe backstop and was okay even though it was inside the city limits. There was hardly any traffic on the old school woods road, and no houses anywhere near so we were never bothered while there.

Target shooting got pretty boring at times and new ideas were always welcome to enliven things. Someone came up with what we thought to be a brilliant idea and that was to shoot at chimney swifts flying over the old school ruins. To do that required different weapons, like shotguns. How we thought it would be okay to do this is beyond my reasoning and that may have been the problem. At times we seemed to have no reasoning ability. Thomas's house, now the First Baptist Church Sunday School Annex, was just across from the school ruins, and just to the east of the McMullens lived Mrs. Pittman, a very nice widow lady. We used our Dad's shotguns and fired away at the elusive birds. I do not think we ever came close to hitting a bird but the birdshot repeatedly sprinkled the McMullen and Pittman houses. This caused a great deal of alarm and concern. Hearing the shot falling on her roof really frightened Mrs. Pittman, to the point that she called the police and reported us. Very soon the policeman, Dutch Alexander, had everything under control. He rushed to the crime scene, confiscated our weapons and took them to City Hall. Our Dads received an extended phone call from the Mayor. Needless to say, our hunting and shooting rights ended immediately for a period of time. The shots were harmless but the idea of shooting in a neighborhood was quite unheard of and was not to be tolerated. I guess we had seen too many old west movies.

The next idea seemed to us to hang on the brilliant side also. Let's blow up balloons, release them and shoot at them as they float away. Great idea, I think C. B. came up with that one, but how are we going to make a balloon go up, air will not do it and we had no helium. Again C. B. had the answer – get some old zinc mason jar screw on caps, cut them into little pieces and put them in a Coca Cola bottle, add sulfuric acid and gas would form. It was wonderful having a doctor's son for a friend. He kept coming up with some pretty high class ideas. Place a balloon over the bottle top and let it fill with gas, tie it off and "wallah!" you had your target. We tried it and everything went smoothly, except the gas did not have enough pressure to inflate a store bought balloon. A brilliant idea, that had it worked would have been a lot of fun.

Later on we were downtown just hanging out and talking to an older friend and mentioned what we had tried to do with the balloons and how they just were too stiff to blow up. He went into the store where he worked and came back with a three pack package of prophylactics and said, "here, try these, they are much thinner and might work." We thanked him and hurried off to get our things together and I suppose giggling all the way knowing what we had and not knowing at the same time. We tried them, for our target that is, and they worked except that we had a hard time seeing them for any distance. We had one prophylactic left and doused it good with mercurochrome to make it more visible. It worked, now we could see our target until it almost went completely out of sight. But that last one ended that bit of fun as we could not afford anymore of those fancy balloons but we did have some good safe target shooting, for a little while anyway.

* Frog Gigging *

Frog gigging occupied a great deal of our time. It first began when Henry Allen, Sidney Johnson, James Medlin, Bobby Hancock and I were messing around and heard the brr-ump, brr-ump of the bullfrogs down on Curry Creek. The first reaction, "hey, lets go gigging." Our first gig was a broomstick and four of the largest fishhooks we could find. Sidney got the hooks from his Dad's tackle box. Mr. Cap did a lot of saltwater fishing so they were fairly large hooks. We straightened them out and spaced them around the end of the stick, securing them with a tack through each eye. Using a lacing technique that I had learned from Britt, we securely lashed the hooks, using braided fishing cord, to the stick and coated the cord with shellac. Dad was Mayor at that particular time and suggested that we go out to the water works and ask the plant manager Harry McDonald to loan us hip boots. He gladly obliged and now we were set, we had everything needed for a good gig session.

We went down the alley between Doctor Lord's office and the Roosevelt Theater and on down behind Ms. Ozzie's house to the swamp on Curry Creek. We found out quickly that only two are needed to successfully gig frogs. Henry, realizing that he did not have a great fondness for snakes, quickly volunteered to stay on land and carry the harvested frogs. I think Bobby did not want him to be lonely so he willingly kept him company.

We had a successful night but learned, if you do not have a sack or a fish stringer to securely carry your frogs, do not hang them on your belt because they will surely get away, cause a dead frog ain't a dead frog till it's dead. Even after they are skinned and ready for the frying pan, they quiver and carry on and rumor has it that the legs will jump out of the frying pan. That is not so, but they will quiver. To sum up that first gigging experience was something like this. Henry, James and Bobby, did not like the environ where the frogs thrived and as far as I can remember they never faced the summertime perils of the swamp again, Sidney had other interest leaving me high and dry. I had to find a good, stick-to-it gigging buddy.

$$\infty$$

Jayne and I began dating in 1949 and at that time her brother Tom and his wife Polly were living with her sister Marie and Bill near Nicholson. Tom and Polly would frequently come to visit his mother and while there would play canasta with Jayne and me. Tom was a good friend and even though he was several years older we always had a good time or an adventurous time. For instance, one of those times we went frog gigging on Mr. Stoy Bell's pond. Mr. Bell was the dad of Bill Bell an old school mate of mine. Their farm was on the Old Pendergrass Road about a mile or two above the P. J. Roberts farm and about six miles from Jefferson. We drove up there late one evening in Dad's old Ford cotton truck and down to the pond about three hundred feet off the road. As soon as darkness fell we put on our boots and began to wade the edge of the pond and after making a couple of rounds around the pond a pretty vicious thunderstorm came up. We tried to get back to the Pendergrass Road before the rain came but about half way out, the ground was saturated and we had a dickens of a time getting out. Our troubles had just begun because the road was not paved and had turned to pure mud. Tom was driving and the rear end of that truck with its tandem wheels was so light there was absolutely no traction plus the tires were too wide to get into the ruts. We were at the mercy of Mother Nature. About a half a mile from the Roberts farm

Tom lost control and the truck slipped into the ditch and high centered with one side in the ditch and the other on the edge of the road. By this time it was getting pretty late and raining like crazy. We had no choice but to get to the Roberts farm as quickly as possible and call home for help. The house was dark and we knew Mr. Roberts had already gone to bed but he answered the door and was willing to help us. Most folk called Mr. Roberts, P. J. The "P" stood for "Pleasant," and indeed he was. No name could fit a person's personality any better. Rather than call Dad and have him come get us, Mr. Roberts knew there was a good chance Dad would end up getting stuck, instead he drove us to Jefferson and told us to come back in the morning and he would pull us out with his tractor. When we got to Tom's house I called Mother and Dad to report that we were okay. I borrowed a shirt and a pair of Tom's khaki pants and Mrs. Staton washed mine. Now that was a sneaky way to ease into the family, wasn't it? Soon after that Tom and Polly moved to Warrenton, Georgia.

A new gigging, fishing and hunting partner showed up pretty quickly, John Anderson. John was four years younger and that made him fourteen or fifteen at the beginning of our friendship. He seemed to be very mature for his age and loved all aspects of the outdoors. He and I had many gigging, hunting and fishing experiences together and he says that I taught him all he knows about hunting but I never saw it that way. All I know is, we had a heck of a time together and I cherish those memories. John became a very successful and noted Doctor of Medicine and is now retired with his new identity, "The Great White Hunter." He goes everywhere, from Africa, to Alaska, Siberia and who knows where else, hunting big game. He has turned into an amazing fellow and it all began in Jackson County. But for now I return to Jackson County as I recall several small game adventures during our early days.

John loved it all, hunting, fishing and gigging. On our frog gigging ventures he would wade ponds and swamps with vigorous enthusiasm, never letting those brown wiggling things in the water or coiled on the banks bother him. One night we went to Bell's Lake and had a very successful night of gigging. It was not a very dark night but it was during the old frogs mating season causing them to be a little careless as they apparently had other things on their mind. In several cases we were able to bag two at the same time. I always thought that to be a bit thoughtless and really not nice. We had a lot of frogs that night and took them to my house to dress them. I never quite understood why you dress a chicken or wild game, it seems to me that it is absolute undressing and should be called such. It was pretty late, around mid-night I think and we were at the back door almost under Mother and Dad's bedroom window. Dad got a big kick out of us as we skinned the frogs and held a pair up comparing them to Betty Grable's legs, like "man these legs are prettier than Betty Grable's any day."

The best gig of all was the time when Wiley and I went on their pond off of the McEver Road near Gainesville. This was during the first summer after Jayne and I got married. Jayne had given me an engraved sterling silver Zippo cigarette lighter as a wedding gift and I lost it overboard that night while gigging. If the pond is still there so is my lighter. This had to be the first time anyone had gigged this pond because frogs were everywhere and it did not take long to harvest over forty large ones. We were gigging from a flat bottom wooden boat and that made it a lot easier getting around.

A few days later Bill, Marie, Wylie, Shirley, Jayne and I went to Rabun Croft for a couple of days. We took the frog legs that we had gigged and had the biggest frog leg fry that you can imagine.

We certainly had our fill and a wonderful time together. Jayne says there were ninety or more legs fried that night.

* Hunting *

Hunting was a favorite for most of the gang. Brother Billy had separated himself from us and spent most of his time with his classmates, Donald Barnett, Dean Dadisman, Wilson "Tick" Wilbanks and others. I remember him going on a couple of dove shoots and Mr. Jett Roberts asking some of the older boys to come out to his place and shoot the squirrels that were playing havoc with his cornfield. I think he paid a bounty of five cents for each squirrel killed. No one got rich and Mr. Roberts didn't go broke either. Billy did not care for hunting very much and I do not remember him ever going fishing with us.

C. B., Thomas and I, on the other hand, hunted squirrels, rabbits and doves pretty often. Thomas was a dead shot when dove shooting. He certainly hit a lot more than he missed. His Dad was the Agriculture teacher at The Martin Institute and later Jefferson High School. His family moved several times as he received better teaching jobs so Thomas was with us for awhile and later gone. I think they were in Blairsville when he graduated from High School.

We did most of our dove shooting at the County Prison Farm. Even though it was a prison, I do not recall any regulations regarding our guns, except when we ate a free dinner at the farm. Then of course, we had to check our guns at the guardhouse or office but on the whole security was not tight at all. Eating out there was a lot of fun and they had the best biscuits you ever put in your mouth.

I remember one day as Sidney Johnson, John Anderson and I were driving on the County Farm Road we saw a large flock of doves, a hundred or more, light in a cornfield that had been recently harvested. The field was a short distance from the road. Sidney had his Dad's short barreled, open bore Winchester pump shotgun, more suited for quail than it was for doves, and he sneaked through the high grass to the edge of the cornfield and flushed the birds. Sidney fired as the birds took off and were about waist to shoulder high. We counted twenty seven birds killed or wounded. Sidney said he only fired one round. We never saw so many feathers flying around in all of our life. He had almost bagged the limit for all three of us with one shot. "Believe it or Not."

Another time on a very chilly morning, John and I were out at the farm shooting doves over near the old hog lot. John was on one end of a cornfield and I on the other. The corn had been harvested and I was hunkered down in the tall grass on the edge and wearing a dark stocking cap. The cap had a white fuzzy ball on top and unbeknownst to me actually turned my person into a decoy. I had already noticed a rather large red-tailed hawk flying around and heard him scream a time or two being quite unaware of his intentions, that was to have breakfast as soon as he could find his meal. He found it and zeroed in on the rabbit sitting in the grass, which was the white knob on my cap. I happened to look up and saw the hawk diving and coming straight toward me, down and in as I raised my gun and fired. The hawk veered off as it immediately lost its appetite for rabbit. John is my witness.

I recall one hunt, a rabbit hunt with John, Wiley and a friend of his who had a couple of beagle dogs. We were up behind what is now the Walnut Fork Office Complex located just across the Middle Oconee River Bridge, east of the Gainesville Highway.

Growing Pains And Gains

The river was up from the previous rains and had flooded the natural swamps along the river, forcing the wildlife to scamper to a higher ground, especially the rabbits or cane cutters we called them. John and I had been doing a great deal of duck hunting and he had hit a lot of ducks, just knocking a few puffs of feathers here and there. He went down to Athens Sporting Goods and bought a box of number two shot, a goose load and an over kill for ducks. On this day in his haste to shoot rabbits, he forgot to leave the goose shells at home and loaded his gun with them. As the hunt went on the beagles jumped an old cutter and through the swamp they went. A few minutes later the rabbit was leading the beagles closer and closer to John and me, we were on the edge of a shallow ditch and that rabbit came running up the ditch at full speed and followed it like a freight train on its track. John got set, leveled down on the rabbit with his J. C. Higgins pump twelve gauge, pulled the trigger and all you could see was mud and hair flying through the air. The poor rabbit did not have a chance against that goose load but it was over in a second. It surely did not suffer.

$$\infty$$

Henry's first of only three duck hunts was the time that Dick Storey, Britt Elrod, Henry and I went up to the swamp just across the old Pendergrass Road bridge. The road and bridge have since been destroyed and relocated. The swamp was on the west of the road and was a roosting place for several species of ducks. We were all dispersed and in our ambush positions, waiting for the birds to come in. Henry was to my left and several ducks came in and Britt and Dick knocked down a couple of mallards. In a short while, Henry fired off a couple of shots and hollered, "I got one!" Well, you do not get excited while duck hunting or if you do, you try to hold your emotions. Several ducks exited the swamp immediately ending that good time. Henry was mighty excited as he rushed into the water to claim his prize and came out holding up a beautiful female hooded merganser, better known as a fish eating duck. We all told him that mergansers were not good to eat as they ate fish and that rendered them to be a trash bird as far as a food source goes. That did not deter Henry, this was his duck and his Mother was going to cook it and that was that.

He took it home and dressed it and his mother prepared it for cooking the very next day. I drove over to Henry's house just in time to see his Mother, with a pan in her hand going back into the house. She had just returned after dumping that half cooked bird in the garbage and told Henry to never bring anything like that home again.

We tried to tell him but you gotta know Henry. When he set his mind on something he usually stuck to it. He was another one of my best and great friends. Henry passed away much too early but as long as there is breath in anyone who knew him, his memory will live on, for there was none other like him.

Bagging that merganser kind of stimulated Henry to go back and bag a real acorn eating duck. Henry was the kind of person always trying to improve things. Like, for instance, shooting ducks with an automatic twenty two rifle instead of a good shotgun. He said," let's go back this evening and I will use your automatic Winchester." I said, Henry, there is no way you are going to hit a flying duck going forty miles per hour and one hundred and fifty feet away with a twenty two bullet – Annie Oakley could not do that." He tried and he did not, but oh well. There was never a dull moment in his presence.

�֍

Then there was the time with Bob Freeman. Bob had expressed a desire to float the Middle Oconee River and jump shoot ducks as they flushed ahead of the boat. Sounded good to me but where could we find a boat? John and I had a previous desire to do that and even gave a feeble attempt to build a boat in the backyard. Bob went a step further. He called one evening and said he had built a boat and for me to come down and check it out. Bob and Betty lived in Miss. Ossie Smith's Boarding house next to Dr. Lord's office.

I went down and he had built a boat about eight feet long or more that looked more like a topless casket, but we both agreed it just might do the job. This happened the year before Jayne and I married and she had given me a new handsome hunting jacket with all the game pockets and ammunition holders. We set the day to go and Billy took Bob and me and the boat up the Gainesville Highway to the Oconee River Bridge. We unloaded and put it in the water and found out real quickly that there was a terrible flaw in Bob's boat design and construction. The balance was so critical a feather could tilt it one way or the other and that was not very conducive to having a successful trip down the river.

The river was up somewhat due to the previous rains but we decided to go anyway, thinking the whole time that we should not. We estimated our time of arrival at Riverside and Billy agreed to meet us there to pick us up. Bob steered the boat and my job was to be the ballast. I had my Remington 16 gauge pump on my left and Bob's Granddad's old hammer twelve gauge was on my right. About half way of our journey there was a sharp turn to the left and a birch tree hung out over the river. I ducked as we passed under the tree but Bob tried to slow us down by grabbing hold of the tree and the boat flipped over. Being in the turn of the river and the fact that the water was above normal, that spot was pretty deep. With two guns and a heavy hunting jacket on, it was all I could do to paddle my way out and I had to let go of Bob's gun. We both got out okay and I took off downstream after the boat and finally catching it, secured it to the bank and went back to where we overturned. I apologized to Bob for losing his gun and we marked the spot with a T-shirt. We got back in the boat and finally came to the Riverside Swamp and pushed our way across to where Billy was. It was after dark and Billy was about to leave to report us missing. We were okay except for being mighty cold as this all happened on a very cold December day.

Bob waited a couple of days for the river waters to recede and hired a couple of young boys to go with him to try to retrieve his gun. We knew that we had to be near the Field's Farm, off of the Old Pendergrass Road. Bob had no trouble finding the spot. He and his helpers poked around with pitchforks for a few minutes and miraculously found the gun. He cleaned it thoroughly and restored it to good condition. That was an amazing outcome to a very scary situation.

We did not bag any ducks and I do not recall even seeing or hearing any. We could not have shot our guns even if we had because we were too busy trying to stay upright. That was our first and last attempt to float the river. It was quite an experience. We still needed a boat.

Another time Billy Elder and I went duck hunting at "The Bends" in the Middle Oconee. Not too far across the new by-pass on the Old Pendergrass Road there was a field road that went down about a half of a mile and ended near the river. The road was where the new sub-division is now, ruining a beautiful landscape. Billy and I had never hunted together and I cannot remember how he was talked into going. We were in Dad's cotton truck again and drove down to the swamp's edge, about an hour or so before the ducks came in to roost. As I recall there were two bends or oxbows in the river and in between those bends were potholes that the ducks would come to. It was getting pretty late before a few ducks came in and we knocked down a couple.

As we were looking for the downed birds darkness fell pretty rapidly and before we knew it, we had become quite disoriented, or a more direct way to put it, we were flat out lost. Every way we turned we kept running into the river. Those darn bends had completely taken control of our lives. We did have flashlights but what good were they except to help us tie our boots or something. But we did have an ace in the hole over Mother Nature and that was the east/west flight line of the airplanes flying from Greenville to Atlanta. The next airplane we saw, with the river to our backs, had to be coming from Greenville. We walked in the direction from whence it came and directly came to the field. The truck was just a short distance away. Now our flashlights really helped because when we finally reached the truck and started out we immediately ran out of gas. It was pitch dark when we started our trek toward the main road.

Jayne, Martha Jean, Henry and Billy's wife, Ada, had become concerned about our well being. Jayne called Dad to find out if I had told him where we were going hunting. I had not but Henry suggested a few places that we might be. Just before Billy and I reached the Swimming Pool Road we saw a car parked ahead between the plum bushes and not risking getting shot or something we blinked our flashlights at the car and they hastily sped away. We figured it was just two lovebirds, doing whatever. Our timing was great. Just as we got on the Swimming Pool Road, we met Henry and the girls and that was some reunion. Jayne and I were newlyweds and she warmed me with several hugs. So far as I know, Billy never went duck hunting again. Not with me anyway.

Sometimes a good duck hunt just does not work out, as I recall the early, cold December morning Wiley and I went out to Dwight Howard's place on the Braselton Highway. John and I had been there on several shoots and usually bagged a couple each time. But this hunt had unknowingly turned sour the day before. Wiley did not have hip boots so I borrowed a pair for him from the water works. I failed to ask him what size he wore and when we got to the swamp that morning Wiley pulled on the boots and they were much too big. We laughed about it but Wiley said they would be okay and we started into the dark swamp. We had not gone far before he was stuck in the muck and fell, getting soaking wet. It is a fact that oversized-doubled up rubber boots and swamp muck could only be compatible when they are not attached to a human foot. It did not take long to get back to the truck but long enough for ice to begin forming on his jacket. We headed for home and I believe that was the last duck hunting that he too, did with me,

Wiley and I had many good times hunting together. Squirrels were always plentiful in the woods down behind his family's meat processing plant and I do not remember ever not having a successful hunt. We had some good crow shoots in the Murphy Bottoms down on Allen Creek and driving the back-roads, stopping occasionally to call a few. Wiley came up with a stuffed red-tailed hawk that we used as a decoy. The crows would spot that bird and swarm and dive at it in a wild frenzy, sometimes oblivious to the noise of our guns. We had several good shoots over the old bird until it could not hold itself together and finally fell apart. The crow was a very destructive bird during the agriculture days and continues its destructive nature today, taking advantage of every food source it might encounter.

I recall the time John and I met Dwight Howard and he took us to a large opening in the swamp indicating that it was the ducks common roosting place. This was by far our best duck hunt. The air was heavy with a light mist and the temperature was in the cool low forties. Conditions were just right for a great hunt. We dispersed ourselves around the opening and waited in ankle to knee deep water. After several long shivering minutes a large flock of ducks appeared. As they dropped down to the pond, we all opened fire and never had we seen so many ducks, dead and crippled, hit the water. As darkness was beginning to fall we abandoned all reasoning and started chasing the cripples, getting soaked to the bone and never realizing how miserable we would be when it was all over. I do not remember how many we bagged that evening but it was several.

* Fishing *

I believe our interest in fishing began during those very early years when we went minnow seining with Doctor Lord, Mr. Cap Johnson and Sam Doster. On several occasions they would let us tag along when they went seining down on Curry Creek on Mr. Tom Davis' Farm off of the Jefferson River Road. It was just a short walk down to the creek. The seining procedure consisted of three people; a seine with two sticks five feet long, one on each end of the seine and a hoe. One person would place his end of the seine on the bottom of the creek and against the bank making sure that the minnows could not get by the seine. The other person held his end out in the creek and just a little up stream making a slight curve in the seine. Another person was the driver and he would move the hoe rapidly from the bank out and moving downstream toward the seine making all the noise and splashing he could make. Just before the driver got to the seine, the holders would drag the seine upstream lifting it at the same time to snare the catch. Red horse and horny head minnows were the most common minnows but some pretty good size catfish and sunfish would be caught along with a water snake or two and that would usually liven things up a bit. Usually three or four sets with the seine would fill a couple of minnow buckets. C. B. was the keeper of the minnows and he would take them down to the school woods branch at the bridge and place the inner core of the buckets in the branch. The fresh water kept them alive and well for later fishing for bass in our mountain lakes.

Doctor Lord and Mr. Johnson would go down to Shellman Bluff each summer and fish for sea trout and sea bass. Shellman Bluff was between Savannah and Brunswick on the Sapelo Sound. In 1951, C. B. reserved a cabin at the fishing camp and he, Billy Elder, Willie Craig and I enjoyed two great days of fishing. The owner of the fishing camp and our guide was a young fellow named Kip. We began each day after having a very early breakfast and Kip taking us out in the shallows to catch our bait which was live shrimp. Kip threw the net out and watching it float like a flat flying pancake and letting it settle to the bottom was truly an art. He let each of us try and I'll tell you now, it is not easy and it would take a while to master that technique. Kip was a pro at it and kept us supplied with all the fresh bait we needed. We had two excellent days fishing, catching mostly sea trout and several different species of fish and that made the trip interesting in itself. I think we counted as many as seventeen species. One little fish was brick red in color and was as mean as a snapping turtle and Kip warned us to keep our fingers clear of its mouth. As I remember it was called a mudfish.

Billy Elder; Willie Craig; C. B. Lord; Harry at Shellman Bluff

When we were not out in the Sound we fished from the top of a bluff casting down into the turbulent surf for croakers. Most of the croakers were about two pounds each and fought like a ten pound fresh water bass. It got its name from the croaking noise it makes. I think Willie enjoyed catching them more than the trout that we caught in the Sound.

Kip could tell by the birds and other signs where the fish were most likely to be, and traveling in two boats, he would lead and we followed. He could also read the weather signs and on the last day out we were completely across the Sound and were catching fish at a pretty fast rate. Kip suddenly announced that a storm was brewing and to pull in our lines and head back to the camp. On a normal day as you crossed the sound at full tide, the bottom was visible. As we headed back the storm hit and the swells over the Sound opened the waters to show the oyster beds, reminiscent of the movie when Moses, (Charlton Heston) was leading the people across the parted waters of the Red Sea. We rode the swells and as we topped over, the water would pull back making us think we would crash on the bottom. Farther in as we entered the channel, a Coast Guard Cutter was coming out and created an enormous wake. We were all worried as to whether we would get back safely. After we reached the camp, Kip admitted that he was pretty uneasy and also said that was the fastest moving storm he had ever been caught in. He apologized for the anxious moments. That adventure ended our stay at Shellman Bluff and a great time and experience. We retired for the night and had a good breakfast the next morning. Kip had our catch of fish packed in ice and we headed for home.

Lake Chatuge at Hiawassee, Georgia was probably the most popular lake to fish in the late forties and fifties. We would usually leave Jefferson about 3:30 a.m. and try to get there by daylight. Then we sat around for a couple of hours until the fog lifted, usually around 9:30. C. B., Paul Ferguson and I went up there on one exciting trip. Each time we went seemed to turn into an adventure. Doctor Lord knew all of the best spots to fish and had given C. B. a mental map as to where they were. I remember the

Glory Hole and the Old Apple Orchard as probably being the best. The lake lies in North Carolina and Georgia and you can fish both states with one state license so long as the boat anchor is in the water and not on dry land. We rented our flat bottom wooden boat for seven dollars and started to the Apple Orchard which was about a mile or two from the landing. Powered with a three and a half horsepower motor it seemed a lifetime before we put the first line in the water. We began fishing, using some of those seined minnows for bait and had caught a couple of bass. C. B. put a fresh minnow on his hook and started his cast. He was in the front of the boat and Paul was in the middle. C. B. held his rod in the casting position and as he began his cast, the hook caught Paul under his jawbone. Paul almost went airborne as he was lifted from his seat. Realizing what had happened, C. B. let the line fall slack. Had he not done so, I feel sure Paul would have gone overboard with the minnow. Fortunately the hook was not imbedded in the flesh behind the jawbone and no surgery was required, allowing us to pleasantly finish the day fishing. Or at least C. B. and I did.

The most memorable fishing trip to Lake Chatuge was with Jayne in 1951. We had been dating almost two years and C. B. asked us to go fishing with him and his cousin Nancy Terry. Nancy lived in Gainesville and the plan was to pick Jayne up at four in the morning and have breakfast at Nancy's house. How we pulled this off is another one of those, "its beyond me," situations. Jayne's mother gave an okay for her to go but her Dad knew nothing of what was going on. When we arrived to pick Jayne up and as I got out of the car, Mrs. Staton said in a low but stern voice, "Harry Bryan, I do not know what has come over me, I would never let my girl go off this early with another boy." Then turning to Jayne said, "be quiet so you do not wake your

Father." I had certainly gained her trust and my love for her grew over the years. She was just another Mother to me and we miss her greatly. She had packed a picnic lunch fit for a king. Fried chicken, pimento cheese sandwiches, deviled eggs and I cannot remember what else but it was a feast. How she kept all of this from Mr. Staton I really do not know but he and I hit it off great too.

We went to Gainesville and had a good breakfast with Nancy and headed on to the lake. I can truly say that the fishing was exceptional and one of the best outings we ever had together. We were using spring lizards for bait on this trip and I asked Jayne to hand me one from the bucket, having no idea she would do it. Not wanting to appear afraid she quickly reached in grabbing one and said, "here!" In other words "here, take the slimy thing and the sooner the better." We all laughed but she passed the test.

It was time for lunch and after making sure we were in Georgia we found a nice spot to enjoy our lunch. After we beached the boat we baited all of our lines and cast them out. As we were eating all four reels started whirrrring. We raced to the boat and I think we caught three of them. I missed mine and ended up helping Jayne land hers. We caught several fish, in fact over the limit. Luckily we did not run into the Game Warden as we were going back to the landing. We headed home with evidence that we truly did go fishing. Mrs. Staton later said, "I must have been out of my mind."

John Anderson and I also had some good times fishing on Lake Chatuge. Usually when he and I went, the heavens would open up with torrential rains and nearly always after we had gotten to the farthermost point on the lake. It did not take long for us to learn that when you are on a mountain lake and hear thunder, you had better head for cover.

I recall on one trip we rented the usual wooden boat with its three and a half horsepower motor and off we went. On this day we were way down the lake into North Carolina and not having much luck at all. Around two or three o'clock we began to get a strike or two and could hear the thunder roll in the distance. We had caught a couple of bass and continuing to fish we ignored the thunder and soon were in the worst storm ever. The rain had a real sting to it as it was driven by the wind. We had at least two miles to go, fighting the wind and the rain. The little three and a half horsepower motor seemed to barely move the boat but after about an hour or so, seeming like three or four, we made it back to the boat landing. We arrived just in time for the storm to be over and soaking wet, we headed for home. It seemed to do that about every time we went there.

John was almost fearless growing up but one thing brought him to his knees. We were fishing in the old Riverside Swamp and John was in a dilapidated wooden swamp boat a good ways up the old river channel. All of a sudden there was a yell and down the channel he came, paddling madly and still yelling. "What's wrong John?" I asked. He yelled, "Get this thing off of me!" It was a leach, normally about a half to an inch long but it had been attached to his leg long enough to be almost fully inflated and about two inches long, hanging off his leg just above his boot. After that experience I kind of doubt he ever used leaches in his medical practice.

Closing that last chapter in our growing up days and our last hunt together was on a Saturday morning, December 19, 1953, the day Jayne and I married. John and I went back to the Howard's swamp. We had no luck, in fact I do not believe we saw a duck but no matter, life was just beginning for both of us. The growing up days were ending and the maturing days lay ahead. That would take us in different directions, to the next level in time.

John and I had many good times together, fishing, hunting, seining for minnows and frog gigging – all in a very short time frame that got away much too quickly. John and Franklin Shumake were in our wedding and the Anderson family moved to Athens just before or after I entered the service. John and I lost touch over the years but have seen each other several times in the last few years.

******

Chapter Nine

School Days

Chapter nine

ON TUESDAY EVENING OF January 13, 1942, Martin Institute was set afire by an arsonist and was completely destroyed. Bob Freeman gives this accounting of how the fire was discovered. There was a basketball game scheduled that night and Joe Griffith and Bob, both seniors, had come early to fire the stoves in the gymnasium dressing rooms. The gymnasium lay just a few feet north of the school. They noticed a glow in the school and upon further investigation discovered the fire. Running to the nearest phone they called the fire department. 17/ The Jefferson Fire Department responded immediately and was on the scene in a matter of minutes. Professors Riden and McConnell and several students were able to crash through a door and saved the school records. 18/ Fire departments from Athens and Commerce responded to the call for help but to no avail as the building was completely destroyed in a matter of minutes.

We shall never forget that fateful night and I, being only nine years old, was literally scared to death. What little boy never wished that the school would blow down or something but this, this was beyond the realm of reality. What in the world were we going to do about our schooling? Our nation had just gone through the Great Depression and now was completely engulfed in World War Two. The people of Jefferson were at their wits end and I am sure many were asking , "what will happen next?"

The Jackson Herald gave this brief description of Martin Institute after its destruction. "The school was chartered as the Jackson County Academy in 1818 and in 1859 the name was changed by an act of legislature to Martin Institute honoring William Duncam Martin. Before his death he willed a part of his estate to provide a school for the children of Jackson County. 18/

The first building, Jackson County Academy was a wooden structure located on Martin Street, where Mr. Staton lived, and burned in 1884. The new Martin Institute was completed on its present site in 1886," 18/ which is now the site of the First Baptist Church office.

Jayne gives this additional historical account of the site on Martin Street, which was her home place. These historical notes are taken from the deeds passed to her father, Frank Christopher Staton from E. E. Martin upon the sale of the property to Mr. Staton in 1946. The deeds have since been passed to the present owner upon his purchase of the property in 2003.

"The land the Martin-Staton house stands on was originally the site of the Jackson Academy School/Martin Institute, now 119 Martin Street. The lot was surveyed in 1888 for the First Baptist Church. According to the deeds of record, the Unity Lodge #36 of Jefferson sold the lot to the Baptist Church on January 20,1894, on which the new Baptist Church was already located. The history of the Baptist Church written in 1972, Age to Age – Our Growing Heritage, states that it took them eight years to complete the building. The new church was dedicated on May 20, 1894. The church met there until 1921, when they completed the new First Baptist Church on its present site on Washington Street.   "The First Baptist Church sold the property to the New Winder Lumber Company on April 24, 1922. The New Winder Lumber Company sold the property to E. E. Martin on November 30, 1923. We assume the church was then made into a residential dwelling.

"My parents, Mr. and Mrs. Frank Christopher Staton moved into the house in 1941 and purchased it from Mr. Martin in 1946. The house had two front and back entrances suitable for a duplex dwelling. They gradually made improvements: under-pinning the house, removing one front door, lowering the ceilings, adding a window in the kitchen and modernizing the kitchen. They put vinyl siding on the exterior and made other improvements to make the house more comfortable.

"In 1991, the First Baptist Church observed its 125th anniversary. As a part of that celebration, members gathered on the original steps that still stand on the Staton property, facing College Street and sang Amazing Grace, just as they had done seventy years before upon the completion of the present Baptist Church.

"My parents occupied the house from 1941 until my Mother's death in 1990. My sister, Frances Staton lived with them and inherited the house from Mother. She added central heat and air in 1998 or 1999 and lived there until 2002." 19/

Schooling continued almost immediately after the school burned as the County and the Jefferson School Boards met and quickly solved the problem of how our education would only be temporarily interrupted. The churches of Jefferson responded and soon classes resumed in the Presbyterian, Methodist, Baptist Churches, the log cabin and the Home Economics Building. Blackboards were installed on the Sunday School walls and back to school we went. This happened over a period of a few short days.

I do not remember much about Martin Institute but I do have a sketchy recollection of how it looked inside. The school lay with its entrance to the west and there were three wings added several years after the school was built. The east wing was on the level of the entrance but the north and south wings each had two or three steps down to floor level. The Superintendent's office was on the left as one entered the main entrance. Our first grade was near the entrance of the east wing and on the left as one entered through that entrance. Our teacher was Miss Sara Wills. The second grade was combined with the third grade and was on the left side of the south wing. Miss Elizabeth Collins was our teacher. Our third grade was taught by Miss Sarah Dadisman and was just to the right at the top of the stairs. There was a big auditorium to the left upstairs and I shall never forget that tremendously heavy, curtain that hung on the stage and sitting in the theater like curved back seats watching as Johnny Mobley performed singing, "He sat on his tombstone and smoked his cigar." I am totally oblivious as to where the fourth grade was in the building but I do recall our teacher Ms. Thelma Thomas. That name sends shivers up my spine even as I speak it this day because I do remember the last few months of the fourth grade in the First Baptist Church. Ms. Thelma was not my favorite teacher nor was I her favorite pupil but I am sure that her reasons for me not being her favorite were far more valid than mine were. I do not remember if I passed or made my rise, as we use to say, or if she kicked me out. But in any case, Ms. Castellaw caught me on the bounce and I spent the fifth year in the bottom of the new Home Economics Building, looking at that bun of hair on the back of her head. The sixth and seventh grades were inconsequential. Mrs. Hewlett 'Boyd' Aderholt taught the sixth grade on the first floor of the Economics Building. Mrs. Vergie Haven, the wife of Reverend Haven, taught seventh grade in the Fellowship Hall of the First Baptist Church and graduation was held in the church sanctuary.

Our first year of high school was taught in the First Methodist Church and the Home Economics Building. Coach Riden taught algebra and science in the Home Economics building and Ms. Ruby Isbell taught literature in the parlor of the Methodist Church. Study Hall was in the sanctuary of the Methodist Church.

There are other things I recall about the old school, some a bit hazy but nevertheless firmly etched in my memory. The school had a large, almost square campus divided by a wide walk, presently the First Baptist Church parking lot. On each end and midway up the walk were brick columns that gave much character to the old school. Pecan trees were planted along both sides of the walkway and on the north and south sides of the campus. They were young trees and did not hinder us from playing ball and games of all sorts. In fact we played in them. There was a playground on the north side of the walk with swings, several see-saws, a high bar and a drinking fountain with a squeeze type faucet. I recall one May-Day celebration on the campus. I was either a rabbit or a rat. I am not sure which, but most likely a rat and that is probably how Ms. Thelma viewed me.

I remember the Halloween Carnivals in the old school. Dunking for apples from a washtub filled with water was reminiscent of drinking from the common well dipper. Everyone dunked and dipped into the same water. I do not know if they ever changed the water, probably not. Another event was driving nails through a two by four. One lick, two licks, three licks earned you a prize. Each event cost a total of five cents to participate. Then there was the marble drop box event. A penny a drop could clean you out in a jiffy, plus the owner of the box got to keep all of the marbles. I always figured that the drop box should be outlawed because many an older boy forced many a young fellow into marble bankruptcy.

Shooting marbles was quite the game in those days. Shooting the "big circle" or the "pig's eye" was the gentleman's way of playing the game as it gave each player the same advantage. There were good solid, meaningful terms used like: no fudging, hunker down, no creeping and my toy. Meaning, "keep your shooter or toy marble in one spot, no fudging or creeping." Hunker down meant, give it all you have, take aim and fire away. You never wanted to be accused of fudging or creeping because shooting marbles was a true game of discipline and integrity.

You never hear of shooting marbles these days and probably the reason is there is not a good place to play. Plain ole dirt is required to have an old fashion marble shoot but these days all you can find is asphalt or grass and neither are conducive to a good game.

The old tin gymnasium survived the holocaust and remained a monument to the school for several years. The old gym as recalled by Mr. Tom H. Cooley, was built circa 1927. The businessmen of

Jefferson began a campaign to fund and construct a gymnasium at Martin Institute. This was quite a community undertaking. The gymnasium was erected using timbers and was completely covered with galvanized tin. However, the structural supports proved to be inadequate and had to be re-enforced to eliminate vibrations while the game was being played. Also the roof had to be raised to accommodate the game. This restructuring took place about 1929. The gymnasium was located adjacent to the north wing of the school across from the old maintenance barn that still stands today. There were no dressing rooms in the gym but were added at a later date. In the meantime, the players dressed and showered in the boiler room of the school. The gym was heated with coal burning pot bellied stoves, located in each corner of the gym. The players kept warm by the pace of the game but the spectators were left to their own resources. The southeast corner of the gym was the Senior Class Concession Store. Jefferson High School continued to use the old gym until the 1951-1952 school year, when a new gymnasium was completed. The old gym was demolished in the late 1950s or early 1960s.10/

✂

We had some good days in the old gym. Almost as far back as I can remember it had been a part of our lives. Playing there on Sunday afternoons seems like just yesterday. I shall never forget the first official game that Curtis Segars and I participated in. Our coach was Coach Riden and I was an eighth grader and Curtis was a seventh grader. We played Jackson Trail and won the game. After that game Curtis and I played through High School. I was Captain of the 1948/49 team and Curtis and I were Co-Captains for the 1949/50 team, my final year. Our coach was Frank Snyder and was liked by all. Along with his coaching and our great team mates: Billy Sailors, Louie Tony, Dick Copas, Carrol Dadisman, Charlie Barrett, Raymond Adams, Sidney

Johnson and Thomas Blackstock, we had a very good team and won the sub-region that year over in Statham. Our greatest win was beating and eliminating Commerce from the tournament. The next year was a great year for the team as I was the only one to graduate and their experience of playing together over the years really jelled. Coach Snyder was hired to coach at Clayton High School in Clayton, Georgia and left the next year.

The only evidence of Martin Institute and the old gymnasium ever having been there are the steps facing Institute Street on the southeast corner and the old oak and pecan trees, standing as sentinels to the years past.

✆

Beginning with the 1941/1942 class our schooling continued in the local churches until 1946 when our new school was finally finished. The name was then changed to the Jefferson Elementary and High School. The Martin Institute class of 1945/1946 held their graduation in the new auditorium but the 1946/1947 class was the first full term to graduate from the new Jefferson Elementary and High School. 10/

A lot of things changed after we entered the new school. Billy was a senior, C. B. a junior and I a sophomore. It was an era in our lives of new opportunities. The building seemed so large with long hallways, numerous and spacious classrooms, new teachers and football was on the horizon. Teachers, students and citizens alike had a lot of pride and enthusiasm to make our school and landscape a place of beauty. Several citizens donated trees and shrubbery from their yards. We would go to the homes and dig shrubbery and transport them to the new campus for planting. I do not remember where it came from but Coach Snyder drove a ton and a half GI truck and would take us out to dig bermuda grass for sprigging our new campus. That was an all time effort, requiring many students and hours to get the job done.

"In 1946, talk began of starting a football program at Jefferson High School. The following notes were taken from, "Jefferson High School and Football-Their beginning-2001." The school board gave the Jefferson Civic Improvement Club the authority to appoint a committee to explore the cost of such a program. The J.C.I.C. appointed Southworth Bryan to chair the committee and consisted of Britt Elrod, Clifford Spratlin, Garnett Spratlin and J. L. McMullen. The committee soon reported that $1,500 would be needed to finance a team. Fund raising began in March 1947 and the committee reported that $1,317.35 had been raised and with the assurance that adequate funds would be received, the necessary equipment was ordered.

"Frank Snyder, Jr. was hired to be the coach at Jefferson High School. Coach Snyder was from Pennsylvania and received his higher education from Ohio State University where he attended on a football scholarship. He served in the United States Army during World War Two and while stationed in the Atlanta, Georgia area, he met Eva Merle Davis. Ms. Davis was a former Jeffersonian and the daughter of T. P. Tom and Zipporah 'Zip' Hayes Davis. She was employed at the Dobbins Air Force Base in Marietta, Georgia and met the coach at a U.S.O. dance. They married in 1943 and after his discharge from the service he entered the University of Georgia to take refresher courses. "While there he applied for the coaching job at the Jefferson High School. He was hired in early summer of 1947. I recall how excited we were to hear the news and even more excited when the coach contacted several of us personally to meet and talk about the football program. In early September the Coach announced to the Jefferson Rotary Club that twenty nine boys had signed on with great enthusiasm and gave a tentative seven game schedule that was later adjusted to eight games, as follows:

October 2 ----------- Jefferson vs Gainesville 'B' team – lost 0 - 39
October 10 -------- Jefferson vs Lavonia: lost 0 – 44
October 17 -------- Jefferson vs Commerce: lost 0 - 31
October 24 ------ Jefferson vs Toccoa: lost 0- 40
**October 31 ----- Jefferson vs Cornelia: lost 0 -7
*November 7------ Jefferson vs Commerce: lost 0 - 13
*November 21 ---- Jefferson vs Madison - unavailable
November 28 ----- Jefferson vs Winder: lost 6 – 25
**Homecoming
*Home games

"Scoring that first and only touchdown against Winder was a victory in itself. You would have thought that we won the game. Paul Ferguson was the hero of the game and the season for that matter. We improved remarkably after the mauling we took at the hands of the Toccoa team and held our opponents to decent scores for the rest of the season. The football program at Jefferson High was born and growing." 10/

We were literally a ragged bunch. Our uniforms were discarded practice uniforms given to the High School by the University of Georgia's Athletic Department and were in very bad condition. Some so bad that the thigh pads were taped to our legs and the knee pads were totally gone from some of the britches. In most cases the stitched belt that held the britches up had to be tied because there was no buckle. Dad and Herman White thought it would boost our morale and they donated funds to buy new jerseys for our game against Toccoa. We had a dose of pride wearing the new jerseys for a little while but those mountain boys beat us up pretty badly and we still had to huddle on a couple of occasions to retie our britches. The next year playing ball in the old uniforms was really pathetic, as you can well imagine.

"There were twenty nine members on the team and later two more joined the team early in the season.

Seniors: Lloyd Craven, Daniel Carithers, James Faulkner, *Paul Ferguson, Archie Lloyd, C. B. Lord, Wylie McEver, C. L. Potts, Roy Smith and *Eugene Tony-Captain. *Paul Ferguson and Eugene Tony were the only players on the team that had football experience. Paul played at Mt. Berry and Gene played at Tech High in Atlanta.

Juniors: Harry Bryan, Quillian Garrison, Joe Glosson, L. G. Jackson, Tom Meade and Garnett Parks.

Sophomores: George Davis, David Foster, Bobby Loggins, James Medlin, William Phillips, Curtis Segars, M. C. Simmons, Claudius Thurmond and Donald White.

Freshmen: Raymond Adams, Dick Copas, Carrol Dadisman, Billy Sailors, Nathan Woodall, Jimmie Doss and Sidney Johnson-manager. "The team cheerleaders were: Jean Ash, Billy Bard, Bobby Dozier, Jane Hendrix, Louie Toney, Betty Roberts, Nell Tolbert and Imogene Westmoreland.

"We coined the mascot name, "Mudturtles," as every game was played in the muddy mire. Mudturtles was thought by some not to be very dignified and was changed at the end of the second season to the "Red Dragons," but now has been modified to simply, The Dragons." 10/

"The history of the Red Dragon is stated in the 1950 yearbook, the Jeffersonian, and reads like this: " Once upon a time the red hills of North Georgia were roamed by, of all things, a Dragon. This Dragon loved the valleys and trees and streams and especially did he love the color of the red hills. He loved it so much that he wanted to change his own color to that of the hills. So one rainy day he rolled and rolled and rolled in the clay and upon going down to a spring to see himself, saw that he was the color of the hills. He was a Red Dragon." 20/

Baseball also began at the new Jefferson High during the 1947-48 school year. My teammates: Curtis Segars, Billy Sailors,

Dick Copas, Joe Glosson, L. G. Jackson, Nelson Tolbert, M. C. Simmons, Bobby Silman and others had some mighty good times playing together for the next couple of years. I recall playing American Legion baseball for a couple or three summers. The first year Curtis, Bill Sailors and I were recruited by Commerce to play on their team as Jefferson was yet to organize a Legion team. Coach Snyder organized a team for the next year. I don't think he much liked for us to play on a Commerce team.

When I recall the baseball days, I always think of Bob (Coach) Ash. Bob married Carolyn Lord, C. B's sister. One day they were visiting the Lords and Bob was outside. He saw me down at my house tossing the ball up and catching it. I must have been thirteen or fourteen years old. He called me to come up and he would play catch with me. He asked me what position I wanted to play and I told him I wanted to be a pitcher. He immediately stepped off the required distance for pitching and said, "let's see what you have." I offered him the glove but he declined its use and said, "fire away." I wound up as best as I knew how and let go with what I thought was a good burning fast ball. Bob did not flinch and zipped the ball back to me. He then taught me how to properly wind up for my next delivery. Bob positioned himself in the catcher's position and coached me for several minutes that day. I shall never forget that day and I recall that many times I would look up the street hoping Bob and Carolyn would be there. But he had done his job by being the spark that helped me enjoy the next few years. He was a wonderful role model for me and to the many young lads whose lives he touched during his long and admired coaching career.

Billy and I spent many hours playing catch in our side yard. I purchased a Bob Feller, How To Pitch, booklet and was able to master several different pitches, from curve balls to change-ups and enjoyed several years playing the sport. Thanks to the two Bobs.

The High School football and baseball practice field was conveniently located where the Baxter/Bryan computer science building presently stands but we had no dressing room. Next to the school cafeteria was an unfinished room and Coach Snyder was given permission to use it for the dressing room. The football players and some of the agriculture students had the task of literally digging it out, moving wheelbarrow after wheelbarrow of dirt. It quickly became known as the Dungeon. Before and while the excavation was going on, the Dungeon was a favorite place for smoking and I shall never forget the time when Henry dropped in for a quick puff or two. It was not only a favorite of students but for some members of the faculty, the coach included. The room was usually filled with smoke but no one ever asked questions. When Henry lit his cigarette he noticed a subdued glow in the rear of the room and said in a low voice, "Harry, is that you?" The voice answered "Henry, I think it best we go to class now." It was Professor Payne and Henry shot out of there in a flash and waited for the consequences. But there were none, as Mr. Payne was also in the wrong and nothing was ever said of the incidence. I sure am glad it was not Coach Snyder. If it had been, we both would have been in serious trouble.   As I was writing the above exploit of Henry, I was reminded of the time when Mr. John Anderson, the County Agent, came to the school to address the Four-H- Club about conservation. Henry and I were not members but somehow got permission to attend that meeting. The war was over and I believe we were in the eleventh grade. I cannot remember who was in the group, but it was all boys. We gathered on the first level, directly above the typing and chemistry rooms. Mr. Anderson made a couple of mistakes at that gathering. He had gotten an U. S. Army surplus "tear gas canister" from somewhere and brought it to the school to show it around. That was his first mistake but the worst was when he held it up and said, "I am going to pass this canister around, but whatever you do, do not pull this pin." Well, when it came around to Henry, guess what? Yep, you guessed it, Henry pulled the pin, there was a click and in a few short seconds, tear gas poured out. You just did not tell Henry not do something. After clamoring to put the pin back Henry dropped the canister and out the door every one flew. Mr. Anderson, crying profusely, retrieved the canister and threw it out of the window. The wind immediately blew the fumes back through the open windows on the bottom floor. That portion of the building was temporarily evacuated, and as you can well imagine Henry spent a good bit of time in Mr. Ash's office trying to explain what and why he did it. There was never a dull moment when Henry was around.

Ironically though, in the early 1960s, Henry taught in the school where he raised so much mischief. I think Mr. Ash's retirement in 1958 made that possible.

Our senior year, 1948-1949 was rather unique. We were the first class given the option to graduate or come back to the first twelfth year. Many of the students graduated that year but there were twenty four of us who came back. Some to actually increase their learning, some because they were in love with a classmate and some to play another year of sports. I chose the latter, plus I too was in love. Jayne and I graduated in 1950, she from the eleventh and I from the twelfth.

There were not many new courses available for us in our advanced year so the curriculum was pretty easy. For instance, mine was eighth grade arithmetic; ninth grade history; chemistry and Driver's Education. Now that was a real scorcher but as I said before, I was in love and wanted to play ball. However, that schedule was enough to offer some pretty good opportunities for mischief, like the time in Miss Rosalind Shepherd's history class. Carlisle Ray had one of those trick greeting cards, the kind that had rubber bands attached to a steel ring. The ring was wound tight, folded over and put in the envelope. When the card was opened the sudden whirrrrring noise scared the daylight out of that person. I asked Carlisle to loan it to me and unfortunately he did. As we were sitting in class, Doris Segars was sitting behind me and I slipped the envelope to her. Miss Shepherd was at the blackboard, talking as she wrote. Doris pulled the card from the envelope, opened it and screamed to high heavens, alerting and directing Miss Shepherd to the point of activity. Doris was as white as a sheet and Miss Shepherd was as red as the Devil himself. Before I could recover the evidence she stood directly over me and directed me to the door to wait outside until further notice. Frankly I think it scared her more than it did Doris. Her color had returned to normal by the time she came out and told me to apologize to Doris and the whole class. Everything went along pretty normally from that point on. Doris later became my sister-in-law.

Many fun things happened during our final school days. I shall never forget the one act plays. One in particular was during our senior year. "The Haunted Suitcase" was its title and it was a part of the annual Halloween Carnival. Jayne was Kay Archer-nineteen, fair-haired, pretty and romantic and I was Jim Irvine – steady but independent and engaged to Kay. Kay and Jim stood before Judge Heron (Jack Legg) at their wedding, as the curtain closed. Those in the play were: Becky (Garrison) Wood, Shirley (Deaton) McEver, Claudius Thurman, Curtis Segars, Clara (Maddox) Segars, Joan Redd, Angie Brumalow, Raymond Adams and Donald White.

⚭

Halloween was always a fun time. It was that time of the year that legalized pranks, or so we thought. Pranks were to be expected and if they were not why did folks prepare for it by taking furniture and stuff from their porches and yards? There was no such thing as trick or treat, it was all trick and if you knocked on a door during Halloween night, it was meant to agitate, nothing else.

The Halloween Carnivals were special and continued on from Martin Institute through our high school days at Jefferson High. They were more special when you participated in them. They kept a lot of kids off of the streets and out of mischief but more importantly, they made money but for whatever purpose we never knew. I shall never forget the carnival when Ms. Ruby called on Claudius Thurman, Bobby Loggins, Henry and me to be in charge of the "Horror House." It was always an honor when Ms. Ruby took you under her wing. The Horror House was in the infamous room where the tear gas episode took place. We had all kind of things hanging and flying around: dim lights, flickering lights, no lights and all kinds of noises of the night, skinned grapes (eyeballs), wet spaghetti (intestines) etc. It turned out to be a huge success and a lot of fun. But a strange thing happened that night. Somebody broke into the office and stole all of the carnival proceeds and they were never recovered. That remains an unsolved mystery to this day.

$$\infty$$

Another Halloween happening that took place when we as Sophomores, Juniors, Seniors and even a college student or two, all gathered to take a communal walk through the neighborhoods which was the impetus for a trick or two. Oh yes, I forgot to mention there was a girl or two along, but no names will be used as it might be a bit embarrassing to some. C. B. was part of the gang, but not a part of the actual mischief. But he was a big part of what happened afterwards. Let me explain. C. B. and his Dad had a prearranged agreement on how to communicate when his Dad had to make a night call to a patient. C. B. would drive him on the call. If the porch light was on, C. B. knew to go home and get the car ready. That happened on Halloween night as we were all gathered together. The porch light was on and C. B. went to get the car. Shortly after he left someone threw a firecracker onto Mrs. Randolph's front porch. Apparently Mrs. Randolph, suspecting trouble had a pre-arranged agreement with Mayor Bob Johnson to have Police Officer Dutch Alexander staked out on the porch that night. He was, and when the firecracker went off the group scattered in all directions with Officer Dutch on the heels of some. Some got away but most of us were not so fortunate. As C. B. brought the car from the garage, Officer Dutch commandeered the car and C. B., unbeknownst to Doctor Lord, was told to drive down the street and stop. Of course, we all piled in. Officer Dutch was in the back seat and I jumped right smack in his lap and saying, "that blankity, blank almost caught me." I immediately recognized whose lap I was sitting in and tried to escape but he wrapped his arms around me and said, "oh no you don't," and carted us all down to City Hall. We were booked and sat waiting for Mayor Bob Johnson to come down. He came and ordered all of us to report to City Court on Monday morning at 9:00 a.m. That was a very embarrassing moment when it was announced over the school public address system for each of us report to the office. We all had to sign out in order to appear in court that Monday morning. Dr. Lord was mad as all get out and threatened to sue the City and I do not recall who got the worst chewing out, we the prisoners from the mayor or the mayor from Doctor Lord and Dad. Dad said, "It is a crying shame that boys cannot be boys and shoot off a few firecrackers. I am going to run for mayor." He did and was mayor for the next two terms, 1949 to 1952 and another term in the late 1950's. I don't think Dad quite understood what had happened. Shooting firecrackers in itself was okay, but on someone's porch, I don't think so. Everything calmed down and life went on after that. The girls and a couple of boys got away clean and their names remain in anonymity to this day and as far as I know there is no record that the event ever took place. So we all remained nice young men and ladies, but the big mystery remains, ----- "Who threw the firecracker?" We all want to know.

Senior trips were special and expected by every class that ever graduated from high school but there was a serious thing that happened the year we finished. The eleventh grade class was looking forward to a trip to Daytona Beach, Florida with great anticipation. But they were told they could not go. Mr. Ash and Ms. Ruby made that decision and said only the twelfth grade seniors could have a trip. That decision caused quite an uproar from students and parents alike. Eleven years of study and they were being denied their rights of a senior trip, I don't think so, and after much wrangling, the decision was reversed and they made their trip. The reason behind their decision to deny the eleventh grade seniors their trip was to coerce them back for the twelfth grade.

Being in love, I had the distinct pleasure of enjoying two senior trips upon graduation. Now how this ever came together is far beyond my reasoning. I approached Mother and Dad with the far flung idea of letting let me have the car for a couple of days and with Henry, Willie Craig and James Faulkner drive down to Daytona to be with Jayne. To my astonishment, they both said yes. I was barely eighteen and still not very wise but somehow I won them over. Probably the reason was, they too, had already fallen in love with Jayne.

The worst things to happen on the trip was James getting stung by a Portuguese Man 'O' War and was rushed to the hospital for an hour or two. And we were almost arrested for loitering as we spent the night on the beach after arriving late that night. The policeman recognized us as being crazy high school kids and decided not to "take us down to the clink." But we always wondered – would the teacher chaperons of the eleventh grade class have come to the rescue and bailed us out of jail? We kind of doubted it.

****

Chapter Ten

Church-Holidays-Scouts and the Fifties

Chapter Ten

Billy and I spent most of our elementary years attending the Baptist Sunday School program and the Baptist Training Union. Dad was a member of the Methodist Church and served on the building committee in 1926 when the present church was rebuilt after fire destroyed the old church in 1925. Mother was an Episcopalian and joined the Methodist Church in the mid-1940s. The Baptist Church had an outstanding youth program and that is where the majority of our friends went. I do not remember ever going to Sunday School at the Methodist Church until I was about ten. Frances, Billy and I were all christened in Mother's home church, Emmanual Episcopalian Church in Staunton, Virginia. I do not believe that Mother went along with the twelve year accountability rule that the Methodist church had adopted and still holds to, but we were confirmed into the church anyway at the ripe old age of twelve. Still not knowing what it was all about, we were brought up believing that the church mattered and would be the backbone of our adult years and that belief has certainly proved to be true.

The years spent in the Baptist Church were very rewarding. I remember the Bible drills, Training Union, and the Royal Ambassadors. I really wanted to be a Royal Ambassador but unless you were a member of the Baptist Church you could not be and neither could you partake of Holy Communion. I recall having my hand pulled back from the juice on a couple of occasions and could never quite understand why.

When Billy and I began going to the Methodist Church, there was a good and active youth program. Barbara Johnson, Dean Dadisman and several more of the older boys and girls had the Sunday School program and the Methodist Youth Fellowship going strong.

There was a good number of kids my age and younger that filled in after they were gone. Our leaders were Mr. and Mrs. Clyde Boggs and Mary Glass Crooks and I would be hard pressed to say how much those three people guided and influenced my life and the lives of many others. Our ministers were wonderful and some were almost like family. The Fowlers, Reverend and Mrs. Barton and Reverend Lamar and Mrs. Watkins were all special. Jayne lived next door to the parsonage and we recall Lamar and his wife, Florence, were very attentive to us during our courting days. We received several cards from them on special occasions, always signed "from one old couple to another."

The church membership was just the common mix of neighbors and friends, worshipping and doing mission work as we do today. There were not as many opportunities as there are today but whenever a need arose, we met it. I remember when we had Stewards in the church and I do not know the wisdom behind why the church no longer has them but when we were growing up Stewards were a very important part of the Methodist system. We were Junior Stewards and helped with ushering, offering collection and any other chores we were called to do.

During the summer months we held many of our MYF meetings under the three large oak trees in the back of the church. Only one remains now, the others were removed several years ago. During our early years the trees always seemed to be giants but now the remaining one is over four feet in diameter and estimated to be one hundred and seventy years old. The site was known as an "oak grove" in the days of William Duncan Martin, whose grave is located on the northeast corner of the church lot and dwells in the shade of the old oak tree. The tree was probably about twelve inches in diameter at the time of his death in 1854, as it stood among the others in the grove.

Many happy hours have been spent under the old oak by the children of long ago and today. The remnants of the old water fountain that refreshed many a young person and adult stands near the tree and is slowly disappearing as the tree gradually encroaches upon it.

We all enjoyed the joint meetings with other fellowship groups. Groups from Winder, Gainesville, Statham, Talmo, and Homer would come to Jefferson and we would visit them. Our members were Janelle Adams, Angie Brumalow, Gay Hargrove, Dick Copas, Sidney Johnson, Billy Wilbanks, Bob Loggins, Bobby Hancock and James Medlin. We had some great times, and as I said before, our leaders were the best.

We had some good times in the youth choir and if I remember correctly, Miss Cathryn Mobley was our brave leader. I think Imogene Westmoreland and Gene Tony carried us through most of the selections we sang, because the boys were in that voice changing mode but those two could sing with the best.

The women of the church in the bygone days had a profound impact on us. Their guidance through doing certainly helped to cultivate our spiritual beings. I can visualize where each family sat on a Sunday morning and at times as Jayne and I sit near or where Mother sat, I can feel a lump in my throat. There were many saints in the generations past who helped make the church what it is today and we had the distinct honor to be a part of many of them. Those were the days when most all of the women wore hats. Some were simple, others pretty elaborate but all were in fashion. Some even looked like they may fly away at any moment. When they were all seated you could see feathers of the pheasant, egret, peacock or some tropical plumage as they moved gently in the breeze of the hand held fan.

This was a beautiful time in our growing up years but a terrible time for our feathered friends, as they were highly treasured for their bright plumage. Unknowingly to the ladies, the before mentioned birds and others were declining at an alarming rate because of the great and continuous demand by the millinery industry for their feathers. Federal controls were implemented to stop the slaughter of that part of the avian world, putting an end to a very fashionable period of time.

I believe the fans were courtesy of the Randolph Funeral Parlor. There were no Funeral Homes as we now have. They were called Parlors, where the body was kept for a short while and later moved to the home of the deceased person. That was the common way to mourn the loss of a loved one and usually relatives and or friends sat up all night with the deceased. I recall doing that on one occasion. Mr. L. B. Moon, the husband of Ms. Miriam Bennett Moon, passed away and Britt was asked to sit with him. Britt asked me if I would keep him company, which I did. I never knew how that custom came about and for what purpose it served. That was just the way it was.

The annual church bazaars were fun times in the life of the church and all the ladies, young and older, worked together making homemade crafts by the dozens. There were Christmas tree ornaments, rag dolls and all sorts of baked goods, ie. cakes, cookies, candy, pies and jellies.

Most all of the ladies belonged to the "Women's Society of Christian Service." That name always had a pleasant sound to it and seemed to really define the work of the ladies but now they are simply the "United Methodist Women" and that seems to be kind of confining. Well, anyway the name may have changed but not the spirit. I remember when it was Mother's turn to host a meeting at our home, and as the ladies gathered they sounded like a swarm of bees as they went about God's business. It has been my experience over the years that a church is only as strong as the women's program, for they are truly the driving force.

The church suppers in the fellowship hall, presently the choir room, were special and even though a little crowded at times were always a lot of fun. Most of the kids and some of the older folks would eat outside under the three large oaks and cedars. There were not many cars, so space for parking was never a problem. Most members walked to Church as that was still a popular mode of travel.

Holidays

The holidays were always special, especially Easter. The ladies dressed in their new dresses and hats purchased exclusively for Easter Sunday. The little ones, girls and boys also had their new outfits. The girls with their long curly hair and the boys with their hair freshly cut, cow-licks included and freshly polished shoes, all looked as fresh as the spring morning and sat proudly, singing along or listening as the choir led us, singing our old familiar Easter songs. Dad was in the choir and walked around the house practicing and driving us a little crazy at times but he had a pretty good untrained voice. On the other hand, Mrs. Howell, our next door neighbor had a trained operatic voice and could rattle the windows in our house. When she cranked up, Dad would too, making us all beg for mercy but when they all assembled in the choir, they blended beautifully. To hear those sounds today would truly be a blessing.

All holidays were special but to our family I think Christmas was by far the favorite. Not for the giving and receiving so much as for the feel and the spirit. It was a feel different part of the year. Mother and Dad made their annual shopping trip to Atlanta, always taking Frances, Billy and me along. Each time we went, it had to be the coldest day of the year and I am convinced that there is no colder place in the world to a little one than a city on a cold, windy winter's night. Walking down the street near Davison-Paxon and feeling the cold air gushing out of the alleys caused tears to form and almost freeze as they ran down our cheeks. But things got better at Davison's windows, seeing the

Christmas scenes of Santa and his elves and the electric train and all of those things that dazzled a little one's eye.

After the shopping spree and as we walked to Rich's parking lot, we always stopped by the Planter's Peanut Shop to buy a bag of freshly roasted peanuts or a bag of mixed nuts. That odor, as far as I was concerned, was the best part of the city and to this day I associate the smell of roasting nuts with Christmas.

On the way home we ate nuts and wrapped in blankets to keep warm. Cars had heaters but leaked so much cold air that the heater was almost useless, especially when you were speeding along at the break neck speed of thirty five miles per hour on the open road. Usually after arriving home, Mother and Frances prepared Welsh rarebit for supper. For those who do not know what Welsh rarebit is, it is melted cheese and something poured over crackers and was mighty good on a cold winter's night.

⤫

Billy and I had the responsibility of supplying the tree to stand in our living room and that was quite an ordeal. Starting a few days before Christmas the tree was found and brought to the house. Next, Billy and I made a stand for the tree, which consisted of two pieces of two by four, crudely notched. The stand was nailed to the tree but it was so unstable it had to be stabilized using bricks or maybe even a piece of wire to hold it in place. The tree was placed in its proper corner on Christmas Eve where it would remain until just before midnight on New Year's Eve. At that time it was taken down and carried outside and placed in the ditch along the street where it was ceremoniously burned. That completed the annual ritual and assured us that the family would have good luck for the coming New Year.

Now, there were two choices of trees, pine and cedar. Mother's choice was the cedar, not just a cedar but "The Cedar." We drove the back roads and whenever we saw a tree that looked suitable, we cut it, and hauled it home. We never thought about getting permission because nobody seemed to care. After all it was just a tree and there were plenty more all around. After arriving home with the tree, Mother and Frances judged it like it was going to be entered in a nationwide contest. They looked at this side, that side, limbs too thin, crooked stem, or whatever. I recall loping a limb off and after it was declared that its removal created too big of a hole, the limb was grafted back using wire to hold it in place.

Man, it got crazy at times. I think if trees were not a renewable resource, Mother and Frances would probably have been the reason for the demise of the eastern red cedar.

On one occasion Billy and I asked Frances if she wanted to go tree hunting with us. That was a real honor for her because tree hunting was a boy's job. I carried my sixteen-gauge shotgun just in case a rabbit or a quail jumped up ahead of us and for some reason Frances wanted to shoot the gun. I showed her how to nestle the stock to her shoulder and she fired away. It gave her a good kick and cured her of ever wanting to shoot a shotgun again and I do not believe she ever again went into the wild to hunt a tree.

After the tree was selected, placed and stabilized in its proper corner it was carefully decorated using ornaments of long ago and always some new ones were added to insure a continuous future supply. The first to be placed was the fragile, little white angel, carefully put on the tip top to overlook the whole Christmas event and to give her approval of all that took place. Each year the little angel continues her vigil on our tree from her position on high.

Mother would go about decorating the house, always hanging a sprig of mistletoe between the living room and dining room. She placed a basket of pinecone here, candles there, and greenery and a ribbon here and there and a wreath on the front door until the aroma and the spirit of Christmas completely filled the house and all who entered.

The First Baptist Church Christmas Pageant, as far as I was concerned, began before time began. It was another one of those things that just happened, a true God given blessing. The Pageant was always special and an important part of Christmas, something to look forward to, to make our Christmas complete. I remember Uncle Morris sitting mostly unnoticed up front and operating the lighting system, which was a couple of tall lamps that were manually operated to be a spot or a broad beam. The colors were changed with different colored lenses and made a clickety clack noise as they were flipped during the events of the pageant and I remember seeing the light as it reflected on Uncle Morris's bald head. And hearing Florence Watkins, sing "O Holy Night" and feeling the chill and the thrill that brought a tear to the eye of those who listened and surely, even the Heavenly Angel wept as she sang. I am sure that is why O Holy Night is my favorite Christmas song since time began and I could not imagine a Christmas without the Church Pageant.

Mother and I had a special rapport and I think we thought a lot alike. This is not to say I was her equal, I was not by any means. For her wisdom was far greater than I could ever acquire. I shall never forget those special times when she and I sat in our front yard and discussed what we supposed each of our missions to be here on earth. I think we decided that God simply wanted companionship and for each of us to be true to Him in every deed. And indeed she was while here on earth and continues to be to Him in eternity.

Scouts

Our encounter with the Boy Scouts of America was fairly brief, lasting just a few short years. Billy, C. B., and Thomas and

Claudius had joined a couple of years earlier and I think the older ones obtained the rank of first class and the younger second class when we all disbanded. We were Troop 65, the Screaming Eagles. Dad, Herman White and Preacher Haven were our leaders in the beginning and later Clyde Boggs, Britt Elrod and Mr. Carlyle took over. Britt was the woodsman of the group and taught us much about scouting. Our members were Billy, C. B., Thomas, Claudius Thurman, Bobby Loggins, James Medlin, Billy Carlyle, Billy Dye and Bobby Hancock.

When we were working to earn merit badges we hiked over to the old track field on a camping venture, that included cooking and the whole ball of wax. Billy and I had gone down to Hardy's Freezer Locker to get a couple of packages of meat from the family locker. Mr. Hardy rented locker space to the people. Billy got hamburger and I got pork chops. Now, I do not know if you have ever tried to cook frozen pork chops on an open fire. If you have not, don't try it. It is virtually impossible to do, but if you have all the time in the world and are not real hungry you might pull it off. Don't try cooking frozen hamburger either. Mr. Boggs got a real kick out of that.

Another time we hiked up to the old Academy Bridge on the Middle Oconee River. Up there and back satisfied our five mile hike requirements. By this time we were a little wiser and instead of frozen meat, I had a couple of Irish potatoes. Britt suggested that I pack river mud around them and roast them in the ashes of the campfire. I think that was about the most stinking mud I ever smelled but Britt said the more stink, the better. Whatever Britt said to do, I did and placed them in the ashes. After an hour or so they were pretty good, around the edges anyway but were raw in the middle. Hot raw potato is pretty good especially when you are hungry. But I came to the firm conclusion that day. "Cooking is best left to the Mothers of the world," and that holds true to this day.

I recall the time some of us in our troop went to Camp Cheunder. I am still not sure where that was, in fact I am not sure how to spell it but phonically that is what it sounds like. I think it was somewhere between Dahlonega and Gainesville, but anyway we were there for a week. Billy had his supply of tasty yeast and we all had our B-B Bats and other snacks plus plenty of chewing gum. Billy woke up one night with a howl. A scorpion tried to share his bed and gave Billy a couple of pretty good stings on his lower leg. Later on I got a dart zapped into the back of my hand between the first and second knuckle and that caused a pretty good outcry. Dad and Mr. Boggs were up there at that time and I think that was the last night to gather around the big fire circle. C. B. and Thomas made the week unscathed.

The Boy Scout Paper drives were always interesting. Sam Kelly's Dad was director of the Rural Electric Association and would donate one of their trucks to pick up the paper. Sam would drive the truck around the neighborhoods collecting paper that had been put out on the street.

Some of the folks would call and pre-arrange for their papers to be picked up. Such was the case with Mrs. A. O. Hood. Mr. Hood was the County Tax Assessor for many years and had accumulated an enormous amount of papers and all were stacked neatly in bundles, upstairs in their garage. The dust was about as deep as the papers but several of us went to work and completely filled the truck from that one stop. We never knew where all the papers went that were collected on those drives but we all felt good, doing our Scout's duty - helping others.

The 1950s came awfully fast, ending the early growing up days. It was now time for college, time to serve our country, time for courting and marriage, careers, starting families and time to find our place in the world. Happy times, sad times and serious times were ahead but the foundation for living those years had been firmly laid and we felt well equipped and secure to meet the future.

Billy spent his first year after high school at Darlington Preparatory School in Rome and C. B. and Paul Ferguson enrolled at Little Emory in Covington. Jayne and I were dating and on several occasions took C. B. and Paul back to Covington on Sunday nights after their weekend visits at home. Billy joined them at Little Emory after a year at Darlington and all three enrolled at the University of Georgia and graduated in 1952.

Billy and Paul enlisted in the army, Paul with a R.O.T.C. commission and C. B. was accepted and entered the Naval Academy. The last person to person contact with C. B. was the time Jayne and I took him to the Atlanta Airport to catch his plane to Norfolk, Virginia. Later in 1953 I wrote him to ask if he could be my best man at our December wedding. Of course, being in the Navy at that time, it was not possible. Wylie McEver graciously filled that void.

All the days in my life prior to 1949 were important but the summer of 1949 was the start of the most important event in my life. It began from Mother's lips, the discovery of the "second lady of my life," Betty Jayne Staton. Mother, Henry and I were standing on the front walk of our home on Lawrenceville Street when I said, "I wish I knew someone to date tonight." Mother answered without hesitation, "why don't you ask Jayne Staton for a date?" My response, "what, that skinny thing." Boy, that was a terrible thing to say coming from a skinny six foot frame, weighing 135 pounds soaking wet. But anyway, the spark was there and after working up enough nerve, I went down to the Joy Theater where she worked selling tickets and hung out for several minutes, finally working up enough nerve and looking into those beautiful green eyes, asked her for a date. She said yes and that was the beginning of a lifetime bond. It was love at first sight and we married in 1953. How did Mother know?

After serving in the Army for two years, we returned home and after finishing school, I began a career in forestry of almost thirty six years, that took us to Mississippi, Alabama, Tennessee and back to Georgia.

Mother and Dad passed away in the early and mid 1970s. The old home place was sold at that time and Jayne and I purchased it back in 1990. After extensive renovations in 1994 we retired and moved back to our beloved home, where it all began in 1933.

****

Epilogue

THE OLD DAYS ARE gone now, almost as suddenly as they began. The way it was, the growing pains and gains, all served their purpose for the times. I am truly honored to have shared my life with the wonderful people mentioned in this book and the many others in our lives and realizing that - some live today but many have slipped away, much too soon, leaving a permanent void in our lives. But as we live our waning years, we can all take solace knowing that our growing pains certainly are our gains and life lives on in the misty memories of the yesterdays and in the brightness of the hopes of tomorrow.

Gathering the ideas and going about the task of putting the past into words, many old friends became a part of the project. A phone call would initiate a visit and the subject of the past began in a flurry of never ending words that all seemed to enjoy. Ms. Frances (Turpin) Ellington and Mr. Ralph were our neighbor for several years and I think my casual visits with her could very well have lasted forever but we had to stop somewhere. Bob and Betty (Hardy) Freeman gave a lot of good information about old downtown Jefferson and their remembrance of the World War Two days. Vernon and Ruth Carter set me straight on several accounts of the past.

Talking about the past inevitably brought up the phrase, "Oh by the way, do you remember such and such ----?" and opening new avenues as they remembered certain situations and confirmed others and on and on it would go. Speaking of one event often gave rise to another and some recalled things that I had forgotten or never knew, awakening new ideas to be entered into the writings.

Brother Billy passed away about midway of writing this book but when he was in the hospital I shared some of the stories, reminding him of the mischief we had gotten into. Stories of the early Isbell escapade, the ducks, the watermelon fiasco and the log cabin adventures. He would give a pleasing smile as he remembered and I am sure, were he here today, he could add plenty more adventures.

Many old school mates, Tom and Martha (Wilbanks) Meade, Becky (Garrison) Wood, Shirley (Deaton) McEver, Ada (Hardy) Elder and Claudius Thurmond all shared their memories of the old canning plant, Martin Institute days and going to school in the churches and Jefferson High School, helping to confirm the facts needed. Ann (Appleby) Jarrett was invaluable in giving historical information or putting me on the right tract to find what was needed. And the time C. D. Kidd stopped by and visited as I was working in the yard on a summer's day. He and I reminisced of the growing up years on Lawrenceville Street, giving rise to many thoughts long before the writing started. And C. B. Lord, my old friend, sent me a copy of his memories of his family during those brief growing up years that added much to this book. Thank you all.

It is my earnest hope that the words in this book will lead the reader to recall and to ponder the wonderful people and experiences that helped to shape his or her life. And remember too, you can be that wonderful person that can help to shape a life. Perhaps you already have.

****